IMAGES
of America

Wilson's Creek National Battlefield Civil War Collection

Mary Cornelia Steele, seen here, was the youngest daughter of William and Roxanna Gizzard Steele. After William's death in 1848, Roxanna married John Ray, the owner of property where the Battle of Wilson's Creek was fought. Mary wed Jerome Bonaparte Yarbrough, son of John Jerome "Rome" and Elizabeth Young Yarbrough, in 1866. Elizabeth was the sister of James Monroe Young, the grandfather of Jennings and Harry Young, who murdered six law enforcement officers near Springfield, Missouri, in 1932, in what was dubbed the Young Brothers Massacre. (Courtesy of Wilson's Creek National Battlefield.)

ON THE COVER: In June 1861, George H. Hubbard, 37, became surgeon of the 2nd New Hampshire Infantry. He was medical director of the Army of the Frontier and supervised the general hospital at Tipton, Missouri. Hubbard (fifth from left) was at the battles of Prairie Grove and Prairie D'Ane in Arkansas. Ironically, he died from an infected left knee, which he cut exiting a horse-drawn tram in 1876. (Courtesy of Wilson's Creek National Battlefield.)

IMAGES
of America

Wilson's Creek National Battlefield Civil War Collection

Anita L. Roberts and Savannah G. Roberts

ARCADIA
PUBLISHING

ISBN 978-0-7385-9106-3

Published by Arcadia Publishing
Charleston, South Carolina

Printed in the United States of America

Library of Congress Control Number: 2011932003

For all general information, please contact Arcadia Publishing:
Telephone 843-853-2070
Fax 843-853-0044
E-mail sales@arcadiapublishing.com
For customer service and orders:
Toll-Free 1-888-313-2665

Visit us on the Internet at www.arcadiapublishing.com

This book is dedicated to William D. Lee, who brought me endless cups of coffee, served me my meals at my desk, and picked up the slack while I worked for months on this project. A book on the Civil War became much more interesting for our entire family when we discovered that William is Robert E. Lee's fourth cousin, six times removed.

Contents

Acknowledgments

As indicated by the name *Wilson's Creek National Battlefield: Civil War Collection*, this book is a compilation of the interesting photographs housed in the Wilson's Creek archive and museum. While the Battle of Wilson's Creek is obviously covered within these pages, we wanted the reader to gain a sense of the depth of the photographic collection available at Wilson's Creek. While focusing on the Trans-Mississippi Theater, which is the overarching theme of the collection, we could not pass up the opportunity to share photographs from other areas of the country. We believe this shows the similarities as well as the differences soldiers faced during the Civil War.

We want to thank the Wilson's Creek National Battlefield of the US Department of the Interior for sharing its unique collection of photographs and documents. All of the photographs and documents in this book are the property of the Wilson's Creek National Battlefield unless otherwise indicated.

The Wilson's Creek National Battlefield staff and volunteers include Deborah Woods, museum curator; Alan Chilton, museum technician; Jeffrey Patrick, librarian; Shauna Kullman, museum intern; and Jane Mooneyham, museum volunteer. Without their assistance, this book would not have been possible.

A special thank-you goes to Alan Chilton, who spent hours removing photographs from their frames so they could be scanned. I really appreciate my daughter Wendy and my son-in-law Seth Hershberger, assistant director of the Cass County Library District, who both read my manuscript and gave me valuable suggestions.

As an associate historian at the Springfield-Greene County Library District's Library Center, I have had the pleasure of working on a unique Civil War digitization project, "Community & Conflict: The Impact of the Civil War in the Ozarks" at www.ozarkscivilwar.org. That project has afforded me an invaluable research resource pertaining in particular to the Trans-Mississippi Theater. I am grateful for the information conveniently gathered on one website from the multiple project partners, including Wilson's Creek National Battlefield.

The information on the National Park Service websites pertaining to the Civil War battles and battlefields throughout the country was also very helpful—especially that for the battles of Wilson's Creek, Missouri; Pea Ridge, Arkansas; and Vicksburg, Mississippi. The facts and figures in the *Historical Times Encyclopedia of the Civil War* by Patricia L. Faust were very helpful, as were the websites Home of the American Civil War at www.civilwarhome.com, www.fold3.com, newspaperarchive.com, and Ancestry.com

Special thanks go to photographers Steven Titus and Steve Ross for their wonderful photographs of the Battle of Wilson's Creek 150th Anniversary Re-enactment.

INTRODUCTION

The Civil War officially began on April 12, 1861, when the Union forces surrendered Fort Sumter, in Charleston Harbor, South Carolina, to the Confederate Army. It began a four-year struggle in which neighbors fought one another, families became divided, and men died—poorly clothed, hungry, and with little to return home to when the fighting finally ceased.

Over 620,000 died during the war's nearly 10,500 military engagements, of which 384 were major battles. The total deaths, from accidents, executions, illnesses, murders, suicides, as well as the Army and Navy combats, are estimated to be over one million. Both armies lost the majority of their men to disease, while a little over 204,000 were killed in actual combat. Approximately 27,000 Missourians were killed during the Civil War.

Most people believe the majority of the Civil War battles took place in the Mid-Atlantic and Southeastern states, but battles actually took place in 25 different states, including Texas and Arizona. Out of all major engagements, 77 percent took place in only eight states, and 50 percent were fought in Virginia, Tennessee, and Missouri alone.

Following the fall of Fort Sumter, Missouri's governor, the active secessionist Claiborne Fox Jackson, refused Pres. Abraham Lincoln's call for troops. Lincoln realized the necessity of keeping Missouri in the Union, because of its strategic location and key resources. Missouri had access to vital waterways, which were essential for transporting goods and men, and it bordered Union and Confederate states, as well as Indian Territory. Missouri's population was the eighth largest in the Union, providing almost 200,000 soldiers to both sides of the conflict. In fact, Missouri provided more men, in proportion to its population, than any other state. Missouri also had industries and natural resources, such as lead for producing ammunition.

In May 1861, violence broke out in St. Louis when Gen. Nathaniel Lyon arrested the Missouri state militia at Camp Jackson. While Lyon marched his prisoners to the Federal arsenal, local citizens gathered in protest, which erupted in bloodshed, killing 28. In June 1861, Jackson and Lyon met in St. Louis, where they attempted to come to terms, but neither would compromise. Although most Missourians did not favor secession, the state was about to be embroiled in four years of conflict.

The Battle of Wilson's Creek, or Oak Hills, as the Confederates called it, was fought on August 10, 1861, about 10 miles southwest of Springfield, Missouri. Wilson's Creek was the stream running through John Ray's property, where the conflict took place. Bloody Hill, where the majority of the battle was fought, was less than a quarter mile from where the famous Wire Road crossed Wilson's Creek.

Wilson's Creek was the first major Civil War engagement west of the Mississippi River and where Gen. Nathaniel Lyon became the first Union general killed in combat. With over 2,300 fatalities, Wilson's Creek had the highest casualty rate of all battles west of the Mississippi River and was one of the longest battles, lasting nearly five hours. The Union forces suffered an estimated 23-percent loss, while the Confederates reported an estimated 10-percent loss.

Wilson's Creek was the second major battle of the war and the second Confederate victory, but the rebels failed to exploit their success by mounting an offensive, allowing the Federals to keep the critical border state of Missouri in the Union. Historians consider it to be one of the most significant battles fought west of the Mississippi River. Ironically, the Battle of Wilson's Creek took place on the 40th anniversary of Missouri becoming the 24th state in the union.

Wilson's Creek National Battlefield began in 1950, with the formation of a nonprofit corporation, one of the oldest private sector support groups in the National Park Service. Its initial priority was purchasing the 37 acres of Bloody Hill, where the majority of the fighting and deaths occurred during the Battle of Wilson's Creek. Another 1,700 acres were acquired with funding from the Missouri Legislature. Wilson's Creek National Park was dedicated on August 10, 1861, which was the 100th anniversary of the battle. A 7,700-square-foot Civil War library and an educational center were added to the visitor center in 2003. Today, the national park's 1,921 acres comprise 80 percent of the original battlefield.

The Wilson's Creek National Battlefield collection contains nearly 100,000 documents and artifacts, along with nearly 1,500 photographs of soldiers and other period subjects. The story of the Wilson's Creek, or Oak Hills, battle is told through these historic items.

The John K. and Ruth L. Hulston Civil War Research Library, located in the Wilson's Creek National Battlefield Visitor Center, was founded in 1985. The library contains over 6,500 volumes, as well as letters, diaries, maps, and government documents relating to the Civil War in the Trans-Mississippi Theater, providing an excellent resource for students, genealogists, and scholars.

Dr. Thomas Sweeney and his wife, Karen, started a museum, which they named for his ancestor, Gen. Thomas Sweeney, who fought in both the Mexican War and the Civil War. In the early 1990s, Sweeney filled the Sweeney Museum with his personal Civil War artifact collection. For years, Sweeney focused his collecting on the Trans-Mississippi Theater, thus creating the largest collection of its kind. In 2005, the Wilson's Creek National Battlefield purchased his collection with approximately $4.5 million of congressional funds. Many battles throughout the Trans-Mississippi Theater are represented in this collection, including Boonville, Lexington, and Dug Springs in Missouri, and Pea Ridge, Helena, and Prairie Grove in Arkansas, as well as the fighting that took place in the Indian Territory, now Oklahoma.

The Civil War Museum (formerly the Sweeney Museum), the Visitor Center, and the Hulston Civil War Research Library house one of the largest publicly held museum collections representing the Civil War in the Trans-Mississippi Theater. It includes an extensive archival collection of letters, diaries, journals, and maps, along with military correspondence and orders covering the prewar "Bleeding Kansas" era, the political and military importance of the critical Missouri border state, and the guerrilla warfare that began prewar and continued postwar. Much of the collection gives in-depth insight into the impact the Civil War had on soldiers, minorities, women, and families.

Minorities were an integral part of the fighting force. Nearly 150,000 Irishmen fought for the Union. At Camp Jackson in May 1861, there were at least four all-Irish militia units. Many Irish in St. Louis agreed with the Confederate cause and opposed strong centralized government, but they supported "armed neutrality." Following the Camp Jackson massacre, many became staunch Confederates. Missouri also had 31,000 Germans in the Union forces. The Turner Battalion from St. Louis was composed of German immigrants, and its flag is on display at the Wilson's Creek National Battlefield Visitor Center.

Native American Confederate general Stand Watie led his Confederate Cherokee Mounted Rifles Regiment, otherwise known as the "Cherokee Braves," into battles throughout the Trans-Mississippi Theater. Confederate troops remained in the field through June 1865, despite the surrender by Gen. Robert E. Lee, on April 9, 1865, at Appomattox, Virginia. Stand Watie surrendered the largest Native American force on June 23, 1865, in Doaksville, Oklahoma. The Cherokee Braves Regimental Flag is also on display at Wilson's Creek.

The 2nd Missouri Colored Infantry—later the 65th US Colored Infantry—organized at Benton Barracks in St. Louis in December 1863 and January 1864. Most of these men were half-starved and, without hats or shoes, were inappropriately dressed for the harsh winter. Many suffered frostbite, requiring amputations of frozen feet and hands.

During the war, more than 60,000 amputations were performed, compared with about 45,000 during World War I and less than 17,000 in World War II. As soldiers who survived amputations came home from the war, artificial limbs, known as prosthetics, became a necessity. Prosthetics were needed for aesthetics and functionality, as returning veterans needed to support themselves and their families. Those who had been farmers needed two limbs to manage a farm.

Dr. Sweeney was very interested in the medical field, and a large portion of the museum collection reflects his interest, documenting the history of medicine and the medical practices of the Civil War. The Visitor Center displays include medical tools and equipment, and a textile exhibit with uniforms, quilts, women's garments, blankets, and saddlebags. Also on display are soldiers' personal items: playing cards, dice, grooming kits, tobacco pipes, and sewing kits, known as "housewives."

On Friday, August 12, 2011, the 150th Battle of Wilson's Creek Anniversary Re-enactment began with opening ceremonies and a morning battle re-enactment. The celebration featured three days of battle re-enactments, craft demonstrations, period food, music and performances, 1860s games, and educational activities for the whole family.

Between 35,000 and 40,000 spectators enjoyed over 200 citizen re-enactors and approximately 3,000 military re-enactors performing a variety of living history events. Visitors came from across the United States, including Hawaii, and from as far as England and New Zealand.

Children took part in the old-fashion fun, with tug-of-war, sack races, and bobbing for apples, as well as a traditional baseball game. Music lovers were treated to fiddle and banjo playing, as well as folk dancers and traditional cloggers. Root beer and other old-fashioned beverages were offered in corked bottles to tickle taste buds and quench thirsts. Modern concessions and a beer garden were also available.

Folks strolled through "Sutlers Row," where more than 25 vendors recreated a "Sutlers Village." During the war, sutlers followed the troops and acted as grocers and dry goods dealers. They also sold the soldiers provisions such as medicine, clothing, writing materials, lye soap, illegal liquor, and a few luxury items. The Western Division of the Blue-Gray Alliance, a re-enactor organization, helped design the battle scenarios and handled all military aspects of the re-enactment.

While the battlefield is supported through the National Park Service budget, many enhancements are provided by the Wilson's Creek National Battlefield Foundation. Proceeds from the sesquicentennial re-enactment directly benefited projects of the Wilson's Creek National Battlefield, such as an 8,000-square-foot addition to house the Civil War Museum Collection. Money also goes toward land preservation, to protect the pristine nature of the battlefield and the rural character of the surrounding area, as well as to educational programs for the general public and over 8,000 students who visit yearly.

This carte-de-visite by J.A. Arthur depicts Abraham Lincoln and George Washington embracing. As he receives Lincoln into heaven, Washington attempts to place a laurel wreath on Lincoln's head. Published by the Philadelphia Publishing Company following Lincoln's death in 1865, the card is entitled *Washington & Lincoln (Apotheosis)*. The word *apotheosis* means "to glorify someone or something, or to elevate a person to a godlike position."

As an early "Free State" settler, Samuel Walker brought immigrant settlers from Ohio to the Kansas Territory in 1855. During the proslavery conflicts with Missouri guerillas, Captain Walker organized the first military company in Kansas, dubbed the "Bloomington Guards," who fought the Battle of Fort Titus, in Douglas County, Kansas, in 1856. Captain Walker raised a company of men in Lawrence, Kansas, for the 1st Kansas Volunteer Regiment, which fought during the Battle of Wilson's Creek.

One

Battle of Wilson's Creek, or Oak Hills

Nathaniel Lyon was a West Point graduate and veteran of both the Seminole and Mexican Wars. After participating in several Native American massacres in California, Lyon was called to St. Louis to command the Union arsenal. Following pro-secessionist governor Claiborne F. Jackson's refusal to supply volunteers at President Lincoln's request, Lyon captured the pro-Confederate Missouri militia at Camp Jackson in St. Louis in May 1861. When negotiations failed with Jackson, Lyon became brigadier general in command of Missouri's Union troops while Jackson was replaced by pro-Union governor Hamilton R. Gamble. This 1862 lithograph of Lyon was created from a painting by American artist Alonzo Chappel, famous for his works depicting people and events from the American Revolution and early-19th-century America. In 1837, Chappel, at only nine years old, sold portraits for $10 each in New York City. In 1849, Rev. Henry Ward Beecher performed Chappel's wedding ceremony in Brooklyn, New York. Beecher was the brother of Harriet Beecher Stowe, author of *Uncle Tom's Cabin*, which helped fuel the abolitionist cause.

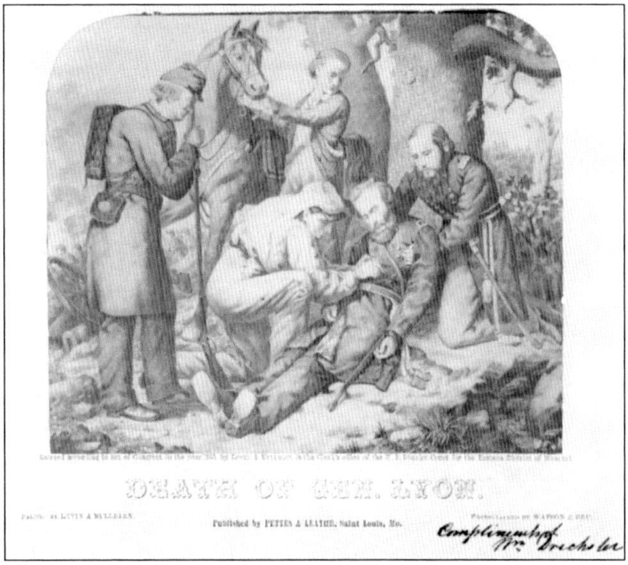

On August 10, 1861, at age 43, Gen. Nathaniel Lyon became the first Union general killed during battle in the Civil War at the Battle of Wilson's Creek. William Levin and William Mulligan's painting *Death of General Lyon* was published by Pettes & Leathe of St. Louis in 1863. Countless renditions of Lyon's death became popular propaganda pieces. This particular interpretation was distributed as a photographic print suitable for framing.

General Lyon was one of the most loved or most hated men in Missouri, depending upon where one's sympathies lay. His horse, Star, raised by Gen. Frederick Steele, became nearly as famous as Lyon. Star was killed during Lyon's first wounding at Wilson's Creek. For years following the battle, soldiers piled rocks honoring Lyon. Some believe the rock pile was actually where Star fell, not where Lyon died later in battle.

William Mackey Wherry, age 25, a first lieutenant in the 3rd US Reserve Corps, Missouri Infantry, was aide-de-camp to General Lyon in 1861 and Gen. John M. Schofield in 1862. In 1895, Pres. Grover Cleveland awarded First Lieutenant Wherry a Medal of Honor for his "conspicuous coolness and heroism in rallying troops that were recoiling under heavy fire" at Wilson's Creek. Wherry became brigadier general during the Spanish-American War, at San Juan Hill, Cuba, in 1898.

In 1853, John McAllister Schofield graduated seventh in his class from West Point. When the Civil War erupted, he became Missouri's mustering officer and major of the 1st Missouri Infantry. Schofield served as General Lyon's chief of staff during the Battle of Wilson's Creek, where he earned the Medal of Honor for "conspicuous gallantry," which he received in 1892. Schofield was buried in Arlington National Cemetery following his death on March 4, 1906.

Pulaski's Light Artillery organized in Pulaski County, Arkansas, in 1860. Originally named Totten's Light Artillery for William Totten, the US arsenal commander, the name changed when Totten's son, James, joined the Union forces. Capt. James Totten fought against Pulaski's Light Artillery at Wilson's Creek. Pulaski's Lt. Omer R. Weaver (left) was the first Arkansan killed during the Wilson's Creek battle. The Omer R. Weaver United Confederate Veterans Camp, No. 354, was organized in 1893.

Before the war, Capt. James Totten of Company F, 2nd US Artillery, assisted with the artillery training of the Pulaski Battery. During the Wilson's Creek battle, "Totten's Battery" dueled with Capt. William Woodruff's Pulaski Battery. Totten's Irish and German troops, in shirtsleeves, repelled assaults by Confederates pushing up Bloody Hill. Cpl. Lorenzo D. Immell, 24, of Totten's Battery, was one of five Battle of Wilson's Creek Medal of Honor recipients.

William H. Merritt moved from New York to Iowa and worked as a merchant, newspaperman, farmer, railroad contractor, and eventually, mayor and postmaster of Des Moines. In 1838, Merritt's was the first mercantile in Iowa to sell to Native Americans. In 1849, gold fever took Merritt to California, but he returned to lead the 6th Iowa Cavalry as a colonel during the Battle of Wilson's Creek in 1861. Colonel Merritt was near General Lyon when he fell.

In 1847, Irish immigrant, Thomas William Sweeny, lost his right arm fighting the Mexican War with New York's Baxter Blues Militia Company. Sweeney fought the Indian Wars and helped to negotiate the Sioux Nations Treaty in 1857. In 1861, Brig. Gen. Sweeny fought during the battles of Carthage and Wilson's Creek. He was shot while fighting under Gen. Nathaniel Lyon at Wilson's Creek and again at Shiloh, Tennessee, in 1862.

Nicknamed "the Black-Bearded Cossack," Col. Eugene Asa Carr led the 3rd Illinois Cavalry in the battles at Wilson's Creek and Vicksburg, Mississippi. Colonel Carr received a Medal of Honor for "distinguished gallantry" during the Battle of Pea Ridge, Arkansas. During the Indian Wars, Carr fought in the Massacre at Wounded Knee, South Dakota, in 1890. He later employed scouts James Butler "Wild Bill" Hickok and William F. "Buffalo Bill" Cody, becoming lifelong friends with them.

In 1861, Theodore A. Switzler and his father-in-law, Robert A. Clark, owned a mercantile in Melville (now Dadeville), Missouri. That year, Switzler joined the Missouri Home Guard and then the 6th Missouri Cavalry, formed primarily of Dade County men. He became provost marshal of southwest Missouri, maintaining troop discipline and administering punishments. Switzler handled deserters and prisoners while suppressing disturbances caused by army troops and individual soldiers.

On March 2, 1921, the *Springfield Leader* reported an infant found on the Wilson's Creek battlefield. The abandoned infant was rumored to be an illegitimate child of a local woman or to have belonged to Southern camp followers. "Eliza" was adopted by the nearby Jones family. By age five, Eliza developed neurological problems and required placement in the county asylum, where she remained. Here, an unidentified woman holds her child in the 1860s.

In May 1861, John P. Renwick of LaGrange, Georgia, enlisted in the 3rd Louisiana Infantry in New Orleans. Soon afterwards, this photograph was taken of Renwick in his Kentucky Military Institute uniform as a gift for a former classmate. Three months later, Renwick became the first of the 3rd Louisiana Infantry to die, while attempting to prevent a Union advance near the Ray House during the Battle of Wilson's Creek.

Unionists John and Roxanna Ray farmed 420 acres on what is now Wilson's Creek National Battlefield. During the Wilson's Creek battle in 1861, the property was bisected by the telegraph-lined Wire Road, which ran from Jefferson City, Missouri, to Fort Smith, Arkansas. John was the area's postmaster. During the battle on August 10, seven-year-old Olivia Ray (shown here as an adult) huddled in their basement with 13 other children; hired hand Julius Short; their slave Rhoda; and Olivia's mother, Roxanna.

In 1837, Roxanna and William Steele received Rhoda, a $300 slave, as a gift at their wedding in Georgia. By 1861, "Aunt" Rhoda and her four children lived with Roxanna, her second husband John Ray, and their combined 11 children on the site of present-day Wilson's Creek National Battlefield. Rhoda Ray (right) tended the wounded following the Wilson's Creek battle. Rhoda lived with the Rays through 1876, before moving to Springfield.

Jerome Bonaparte Yarbrough of Springfield, Missouri, became first lieutenant of the 24th Missouri Infantry Volunteers in 1861. On July 22, 1866, Yarbrough, 29, married Mary Cornelia Steele, 18, the "Ray House" daughter of Roxanna Grizzard Steele Ray and her first husband, William Steele. Following the war, Jerome and Mary raised 15 children on 120 acres in Greene County, Missouri, where Jerome served two terms as deputy sheriff.

Ohio lawyer Robert Byington Mitchell served in the Mexican and Civil Wars. He represented the Kansas Free-State Party as treasurer from 1859 to 1861. Mitchell formed the 2nd Kansas Infantry in 1861, which fought with Gen. Nathaniel Lyon's Army of the West at Wilson's Creek. As the last regiment off the battlefield, they were dubbed the "Bloody Second." Mitchell was severely wounded at Wilson's Creek, but he went on to become territorial governor of New Mexico.

In 1882, John T. Nelson of Christian County, Missouri, sits in the foreground as Rev. Lycurgus J. Baughman leans on the gate next to the new Ray House owner, James M. Rvrie, beside an unidentified woman sitting on the fence. Behind them, from left to right, are two unidentified men, John McConnell, who purchased Ray House in 1905, and an unidentified woman. McConnell's daughter, Bessie McElhaney, owned the house when Wilson's Creek National Battlefield was established in 1960.

During August 8–10, 1901, the Confederate Reunion Convention was held in Springfield, Missouri. On the first day, delegates assembled at the Baldwin Theater on St. Louis Street, where Springfield's acting mayor, Chilton Atkinson, and Missouri governor Alex M. Dockery gave speeches. The Hobart Military Band played musical selections, but the highlight of the convention was the unveiling of the Gen. Sterling Price Confederate Monument at the newly dedicated Springfield National Cemetery.

Two

Battles, Skirmishes, and Other Engagements

In 1851, Karoly "Charles" D. Zagonyi left his native Hungary (now Romania), becoming a naturalized US citizen in 1860. In July 1861, the former captain of hussars enlisted under Gen. John C. Fremont, the Union commander in Missouri. On October 25, Major Zagonyi and 300 of "Fremont's Body Guard" charged 1,500 Missouri state guardsmen near Springfield. The Confederate's had their flag raised above the courthouse in the Public Square, but Fremont's Body Guard galloped into town, freeing Union prisoners and encouraging local Unionists. The Confederate flag was torn down and Springfield's Dr. Samuel H. Melcher quickly replaced it with a Union flag. Zagonyi and his men retreated, but their actions became known as "Zagonyi's Charge" or "Zagonyi's Death Raid." Zagonyi became colonel of the US Volunteers in March 1862, and he resigned in June 1864. In 1854, Zagonyi had married Amanda Speer in Manhattan, and they had a son, Charles Jr., in 1869. Zagonyi Sr. may have died in 1869, but rumors claim he returned to Hungary. The 10.5-acre Zagonyi Park in Springfield memorializes him.

After the First Battle of Springfield, or Zagonyi's Charge, on October 25, 1861, Col. Clark Wright (left) and the 6th Missouri Cavalry held Springfield while 15,000 Union troops retreated to Rolla, Missouri. Then, Wright escorted 276 wagons full of citizens and 30 commissary wagons to Rolla, with 12,000 rebels pursuing them. Wright, dubbed the "dashing cavalryman," participated in battles at Wilson's Creek, Pea Ridge, and Vicksburg.

Civil War forts were usually built on high ground, near water and main roads. After Springfield became a Union military depot in February 1862, construction of five forts was planned. The largest, Fort No. 1, contained a dirt parapet, log walls supported by posts, and two brass six-pounder field pieces. During the Battle of Springfield on January 8, 1863, Fort No. 1 was Springfield's last line of defense.

Hungarian immigrant Alexander Sandor Asboth became Gen. John C. Fremont's chief of staff in 1861. Known for his huge drooping mustache, General Asboth was wounded during the Battle of Pea Ridge in 1862 and shot in his cheek during the Battle of Marianna, Florida, in 1864. After the war, Asboth was appointed US minister to Argentina and Uruguay in 1866, and he died in Buenos Aires in 1868.

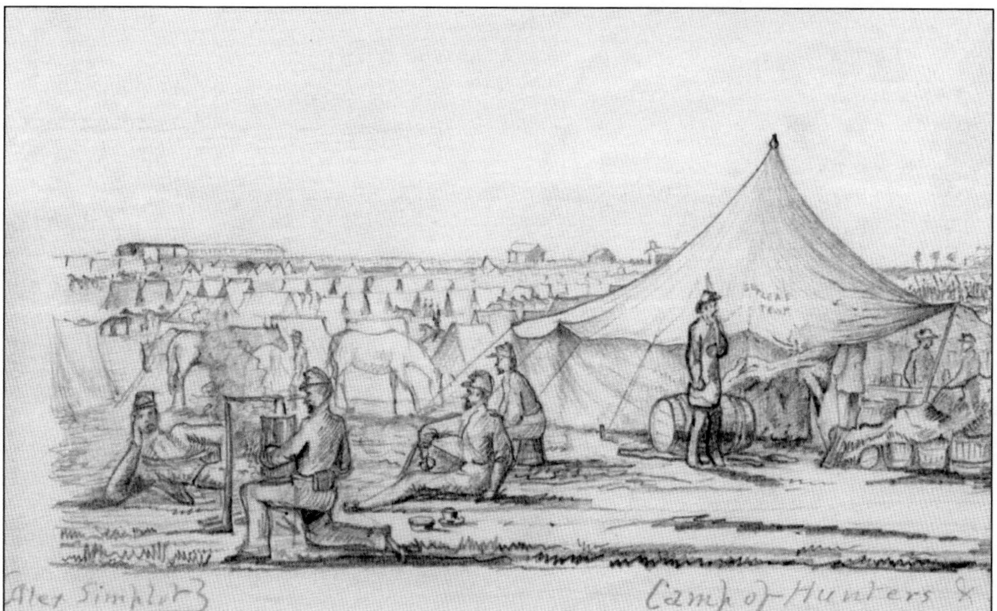

In 1861, pencil artist Alexander Simplot joined 500 correspondents of the "Bohemian Brigade," covering the war in words and images. *Harper's Weekly* paid Simplot $1,250 for 50 drawings. Simplot drew the Union Army divisions of generals David Hunter and Alexander S. Asboth at Tipton, Missouri. On the back, Simplot stated to *Harper's Weekly* that 10,000 men were located on the Pacific Railroad. After the war, Simplot became a lithographer in Dubuque, Iowa.

Just before his death at the Battle of Wilson's Creek, Gen. Nathaniel Lyon authorized Col. Sempronius H. Boyd to organize the 24th Missouri Infantry in Greene County, Missouri, which was nicknamed "Lyon's Legion." Prominent Springfield lawyer and president of the Springfield Wagon Company "Pony" Boyd was also a congressman and one of Missouri's antislavery politicians. In 1890, Pres. Benjamin Harrison appointed Boyd minister and consul general to Siam.

Christopher C. Auger graduated from West Point in 1843, along with three future Confederate generals and 10 future Union generals, including future Pres. Ulysses S. Grant. Auger served in the Mexican War, the Indian Wars, and the Siege of Port Hudson, Louisiana. He was also with President Lincoln at Peterson House following Lincoln's fatal shooting on April 14, 1865, and supervised the removal of his body to the White House.

These "ratholes" were dug into the dirt walls of the Confederate fortifications at the Battle and Siege of Port Hudson, Louisiana, which began May 27, 1863. At Port Hudson, black soldiers attacked with the regular US Army for the first time. The rebels escaped the Yankee artillery shell bombardments by hunkering down inside these earthworks until the siege ended July 9, 1863. Toward the end, the rebels ate horses, mules, dogs, and even rats.

FARRAGUT ON THE HARTFORD AT MOBILE BAY AUGUST 5, 1864

At nine years old, James Glasgow Farragut took the first name of his guardian, Comdr. David Porter, becoming "David" Glasgow Farragut. Here, Farragut and his men are depicted aboard USS *Hartford*, which charged the torpedo-filled Mobile Bay. USS *Tecumseh* struck a torpedo (now called mines) and sank, but Farragut urged his men to victory, reportedly shouting the famous phrase, "Damn the torpedoes! Full speed ahead!" Farragut became the US Navy's first full admiral and his hometown was renamed Farragut, Tennessee.

Gen. John C. Pemberton left the Union Army in 1861, joining the Confederacy to support his Virginia-born wife, Martha "Pattie" Thompson. Eventually, he commanded the Department of Mississippi, including Vicksburg, the last Confederate obstacle to Union shipping on the Mississippi River. Following a 48-day siege, Pemberton surrendered Vicksburg to Union general Ulysses S. Grant on July 4, 1863. Fourth of July celebrations were not held in Vicksburg for another 81 years.

Born to an Army officer in the Choctaw Indian Territory in 1835, Frank Crawford Armstrong became a Union captain in 1861, with the 2nd Cavalry at Fort Leavenworth, Kansas. Armstrong quickly switched sides, and in 1862, he fought under Confederate generals James McQueen McIntosh and Benjamin McCulloch, who died during the Battle of Pea Ridge, Arkansas. In 1863, Colonel Armstrong married Maria Polk Walker, the great-niece of Pres. James Knox Polk.

Union colonel John McNeil, leading 1,000 men of the 2nd Missouri Cavalry, pursued Col. Joseph C. Porter and 2,500 of his Confederate Missouri Brigade for over a week. On April 6, 1862, they finally caught up to them, and a battle erupted at Kirksville, Missouri. McNeil attacked Porter and his men, who were hidden in homes, stores, and fields. The Union victory consolidated Federal control over northeast Missouri, but McNeil was criticized for 15 hasty executions.

This drawing depicts the northwest Arkansas Battle of Pea Ridge, including Samuel Pratt's Pea Ridge store. It was located on Wire Road, otherwise known as Telegraph Road, between Elkhorn Tavern and Little Sugar Creek. Pratt's Store was the hub of Union activity, with Gen. Samuel R. Curtis's headquarters tent pitched nearby. Following the battle, a makeshift tent hospital was set up around Pratt's Store to accommodate the overflow of wounded soldiers.

Proslavery Kentuckian Robert Anderson was an 1825 West Point graduate and loyal Unionist. He was related to William Clark of the Lewis and Clark Expedition, as well as Montgomery Blair, a member of President Lincoln's cabinet who was abolitionist John Brown's attorney following the Harper's Ferry, Virginia, raid. Major Anderson commanded South Carolina's Charleston Harbor for the Union during the 1860 secession crisis. He was photographed in February 1861, while garrisoned at Fort Sumter, South Carolina, prior to the bombardment by secessionist forces on April 12–13. Even though over 3,000 shots hit the fort, Anderson salvaged Fort Sumter's flag when forced to surrender to the Confederates. After Charleston's recapture in 1865, Anderson raised the same flag during the ceremony depicted below. In 1871, Anderson was buried with the Fort Sumter flag as a winding-sheet.

In 1861, Confederate sympathizer and Ozarks physician Beverly A. Barrett treated both rebel and Yankee patients. In 1863, Capt. Joseph G. Peevy of the 11th Missouri Infantry, former sheriff of Barry County, Missouri, was jailed as a convicted Confederate spy in Springfield, Missouri. Theodosia Smith, a Springfield widow, sprang Peevy, with Barrett's assistance, by impersonating the colonel of the 5th Kansas Cavalry, who was the Springfield Military Post commander.

Alexander Simplot's *Plaza at Springfield* appeared in *Harper's Weekly* on November 30, 1861. This image depicts the 1858 flag-topped Greene County Courthouse being used as a Union hospital. The 1837 brick courthouse (center) burned on October 28, 1861. Simplot became a well-known pencil artist, whom *Harper's Weekly* hired to capture the Civil War. He was the only artist covering the Battle of Memphis, Tennessee, on June 6, 1862.

The 292-day siege of Petersburg, Virginia, from June 1864 to April 1865, was one of the last Eastern Theater campaigns. Petersburg's strategically located supply depot was critical to the Confederacy. On June 18, the 1st Maine Heavy Artillery had 635 out of 900 men killed or wounded within seven minutes of the battle beginning. The Union losses were estimated at upwards of 42,000, while Confederate losses were estimated at 28,000.

Five years after the first Blue-Gray Reunion in Springfield, Missouri, approximately 1,000 veterans attended this 1883 reunion. Attendees received half-price fares from several railroad companies. Buildings were decorated with bunting, flags, and soldier's portraits, and the activities included a reception, entertainment, and a military camp. Union generals Franz Sigel, John B. Clark Jr., and John Schofield were in attendance as well as Confederate generals Nicholas "Bart" Pearce, Thomas Churchill, and Louis Hébert.

Three

Military Posts and Other Interesting Places

This 1861 memorial collage of the Marshall House in Alexandria, Virginia, is by Civil War photographer Mathew Brady. It was published by E. Anthony in New York City, who was known for producing Brady's images. This collage honors Elmer Ephraim Ellsworth, who was dubbed "the Martyr." Ellsworth organized the US Zouave Cadets militia unit in Chicago and became friends with Abraham Lincoln while working on his 1860 presidential campaign. In 1861, Ellsworth answered Lincoln's call for 75,000 state militiamen by forming the 11th New York Infantry. On May 24, 1861, Colonel Ellsworth was shot and killed by innkeeper James W. Jackson, after he removed a Confederate flag that was flying above Jackson's inn, the Marshall House. Cpl. Francis E. Brownell fatally shot Jackson in retaliation. Ellsworth became the first Union casualty of the Civil War, and his body was removed to the White House, where President Lincoln was deeply affected by his close friend's death. "Remember Ellsworth!" became a Union rallying cry, while Jackson's legend was celebrated in the 1862 book *Life of James W. Jackson, The Alexandria Hero.*

In the winter of 1864, Union general Joseph Hooker poses with other generals and his staff in front of the canvas-roofed cabins in his "log city" in Lookout Valley, Tennessee. Pictured are, from left to right, Capt. James A. Hall, unidentified, Gen. John White Geary, Gen. Daniel Butterfield, unidentified, Gen. Hooker, unidentified, Gen. William LeDuc, two unidentified, and Hooker's adjutant general, Capt. Charles H. Kibler of the 66th Ohio Infantry.

Federal troops were stationed at DeValls Bluff, Arkansas, following the Confederates' loss of Little Rock to Union forces in September 1863. Stern-wheel and side-wheel army transports are shown at the DeValls Bluff landing, which played an important part in transporting Union troops into Arkansas. The Federals relocated buildings from Des Arc, Arkansas, to DeValls Bluff. Fireplaces and chimneys were constructed out of bricks from the destroyed courthouse in Clarendon, Arkansas.

In June 1864, Civil War photographer Matthew Brady photographed Gen. David McMurtrie Gregg (seated, right, with the beard) under the flag of the 2nd Division of the Army of the Potomac—along with 1st Lt. Albert M. Harper (standing, far left) of the 139th Pennsylvania Infantry, Medal of Honor recipient Capt. Henry C. Wein, Capt. Charles Treichel of the 60th Pennsylvania Volunteers, Col. Charles Taylor of the 1st Pennsylvania Rifles, and two unidentified officers. In 1874, President Grant appointed Gregg US consul to Prague.

Named for New York congressman John A. Griswold, the 21st New York (Griswold) Cavalry defended Washington, DC, in 1863. In 1864, Capt. James S. Graham of Company H (left, with whip) poses with these unidentified cavalrymen at their winter quarters in Winchester, Virginia. These winter camps were built of logs with mud chinking and generally featured a fireplace. In mid-1866, the 21st New York Cavalry was assigned to the Department of Missouri.

This Civil War–era photograph shows a camp full of Sibley tents, which were invented by Brig. Gen. Henry Hopkins Sibley and patented in 1856. Standing 12 feet tall and 18 feet in diameter, the conical design comfortably housed 12 men. In 1858, the Department of War offered Sibley $5 a tent, but he resigned from the Union Army to join the Confederacy. Nearly 44,000 Sibley tents were used during the war.

US congressman Cadwallader Colden Washburn was also Wisconsin governor and founder of the Minneapolis Milling Company (later General Mills). When the war began, Colonel Washburn organized the 2nd Wisconsin Cavalry at Camp Washburn, in Milwaukee. Within two weeks, it left for Benton Barracks in St. Louis, where soldiers drew horses and equipped for the field. The 1st Battalion of the 2nd Wisconsin Cavalry is lined up at Benton Barracks in this 1862 photograph.

In 1862, Col. William Dewey, Col. William H. Kinsman, Col. Samuel L. Glasgow, Lt. Col. Charles J. Clark, and Maj. Leonard B. Houston organized the 23rd Iowa Infantry at Camp Burnside, in Des Moines. Here, a group of 23rd Iowa Infantrymen poses at an officer's quarters. In Missouri, they served on provost duty. Although sickness prevailed throughout the regiment, it fought most Mississippi battles, including Port Gibson, Big Black River Bridge, and Vicksburg.

Founded in July 1869, Pleasanton, Kansas, was named for Gen. Alfred Pleasanton, Union cavalry commander during the Mine Creek battle on October 25, 1864, which resulted in over 400 casualties and the capture of Confederate generals John S. Marmaduke and William L. Cabell. The Battle of Mine Creek, also called the Battle of the Osage, was the only major battle in Kansas and one of the largest cavalry battles of the Civil War.

In 1819, Ezra Fox became the first white settler in Monroe County, Missouri. In 1831, his son, Josephus C. Fox, donated land for the town of Paris, which was named for his wife's hometown of Paris, Kentucky. This photograph of Paris, Missouri, shows Boon and Buchner Mercantile, which was co-owned by William F. Buckner, a merchant and Paris National Bank president, who lived to be 101 years old. Samuel Clemens—or Mark Twain—was born in nearby Florida, Missouri.

Built in 1855, this undated photograph shows the 31-room Glenn House in Paris, Missouri. The exterior walls were made of 14-inch-thick red bricks. Hotel facilities were above the main floor, which housed a drugstore, café, and cigar factory. During the Civil War, soldiers made Glenn House their headquarters. After the war, social events were held there for over 75 years. It was renamed the Jefferson Hotel and was razed in 1974, after 119 years.

Henry Leavenworth established Cantonment Leavenworth on the Missouri River in 1827. It became Fort Leavenworth when eastern Indian tribes were forced west during Pres. Andrew Jackson's Indian Removal Act of 1830. Fort Leavenworth served as an arsenal and troop post dedicated to protecting fur trade, preserving peace among Indian tribes, and safeguarding the Santa Fe Trail commerce. Fort Leavenworth is the oldest active Army post west of the Mississippi River.

Pontoon bridges were used extensively by both armies. These temporary bridges used pontoons, which were flat-bottomed wooden boats, covered with planks called chess boards. Nails were never used so they could be quickly dismantled. In June 1864, Gen. Ulysses S. Grant and the Army of the Potomac crossed the James River at Weyanoke Point, Virginia, using this pontoon bridge, which was the war's longest constructed bridge. This 2,200-foot bridge was built in five hours and dismantled in four days.

During the Siege of Vicksburg, from May 22, 1963, to July 4, 1863, Gen. Ulysses S. Grant used Helena, Arkansas, as an important Mississippi River logistics base. Gen. John C. Pemberton surrendered Vicksburg on July 4, 1863, while Helena fought one of the largest and bloodiest battles of the Trans-Mississippi Theater. In 1864, six Union picket guards float on a flatboat with a mounted howitzer during a flood in Helena.

Shown here in 1865, the Helena, Arkansas, cotton market was a hotbed of activity and disease. During more than three years of Union occupation, Helena became one of the Union's unhealthiest sites. By January 1865, Maj. Gen. Henry W. Halleck recommended abandoning the disease-ridden town. Men blamed the camps' unhealthiness on the officers, particularly Maj. Gen. Samuel R. Curtis, who seemed more interested in cotton speculation than the well-being of his troops.

The 3rd Arkansas Infantry (African Descent), later the 56th US Colored Troops, was Missouri's first black regiment. Composed of Missouri's freemen and the slaves of loyal Unionists, the infantry organized at Schofield Barracks in St. Louis during August 1863. By September 1866, it had lost 43 percent of its 1,583 men, mostly to disease, while serving garrison duty in Helena, Arkansas. Helena's provost marshal's office was a recruiting station and a "safe haven" for runaway slaves.

The guns of the Union Navy at Battery Marshall on tiny Sullivan's Island, South Carolina, were pointed northeast toward any Confederate ships maneuvering along the coast. Battery Marshall was one of several smaller forts on the island, which also housed the larger Fort Moultrie. In February 1864, *H.L. Hunley*, a Confederate submersible, passed below Battery Marshall through the channel to sink USS *Housatonic* during the first successful submarine attack in history.

Libby Prison was constructed by John Enders Sr., the founder of the tobacco industry in Richmond, Virginia, and purchased by Capt. Luther Libby in 1854. Beginning in 1862, over 50,000 Union prisoners, spies, and slaves passed via the Confederate Libby Prison. In 1864, 109 Union officers escaped through a tunnel, but 48 were recaptured and 2 drowned. Shown here in 1865, Libby Prison was dismantled in 1888 and relocated to Chicago to become a museum.

In August 1861, the 26th Illinois Infantry organized at Camp Butler near Springfield, Illinois. Traveling without arms, clothing, or blankets, the men spent a miserable fall and winter fighting bushwhackers while guarding the St. Joseph Railroad and Hannibal, Missouri. Charles F. Wightman, Musician of Company C, sketched a picture of Camp Loomis at Hannibal, which Gibson and Company of Cincinnati, Ohio, then made into this lithograph. Wightman's wartime artwork now sells for $850 or more.

Originally named Hiram Ulysses Grant (a West Point error changed Grant's name forever), Ulysses S. Grant died on July 23, 1885, of throat cancer. On August 8, 1885, memorial services were held throughout the northern states, and in many southern towns, to commemorate the Union general and two-term US president. Joseph E. Johnson traveled from Portland, Oregon, to act as pallbearer beside fellow former Confederate general Simon B. Buckner and Union generals William T. Sherman and Philip H. Sheridan. At least 200 Confederate officers were in attendance. More than 275,000 people viewed Grant's remains in New York City Hall—with many waiting over eight hours to do so. Grant's funeral procession and ceremonies were viewed by 1.5 million people. In the Hudson River, five warships and the US Revenue Cutter Service vessel *Grant*—often called *U.S. Grant*—performed naval ceremonies. At dawn, the bells tolled and cannons boomed in New York, but the sound echoed across the country following the notification by Western Union Telegraph Company that Grant's burial ceremony had begun at 9:45 a.m.

The Springfield National Cemetery, shown here, began with the reburial of 800 casualties from the Wilson's Creek and Springfield battles in 1867. The cemetery holds the remains of one Revolutionary War soldier, five Medal of Honor recipients, five US Army "Buffalo Soldiers," one Civil War nurse, and one three-war veteran. The Springfield Cemetery and the neighboring Confederate Cemetery were merged in 1911.

In 1871, the 6.3-acre Confederate Cemetery was established by the Confederate Cemetery Association in Springfield, Missouri. Former Confederates decorated gravesites in June 1890. In 1901, the United Confederate Veterans of Missouri hired Italian sculptor Chevalier Trentanove to produce a bronze monument honoring Confederate general Sterling Price. Trentanove was the son-in-law of Kentucky senator Joseph C.S. Blackburn, who laid the cornerstone for the Lincoln Memorial in Washington, DC, in 1915.

Four

MEDICAL CARE, BATTLE WOUNDS, AND DISEASES

This staged amputation scene was typical of 75% of all operations performed by Civil War surgeons. Three out of four wounded soldiers were hit in their extremities, making amputation the only viable medical treatment. Approximately 60,000 amputations were performed during the war. The survival rate was higher when surgery was performed within 48 hours of injury. Experienced surgeons could remove a limb within a few minutes, but many doctors were inexperienced—many having never seen inside a living person, treated a gunshot wound, or performed an amputation. A few surgeons in medical institutions had performed amputations for accident injuries or bone tumor removal, but many medical students at that time never even graduated. Located at the rear of the battlefield, the surgeon and usually two assistants generally performed surgeries outdoors to take advantage of the daylight, which was brighter than candles or kerosene lamps. Unfortunately, they used the same instruments all day, without any thought to sterilizing them or washing their hands. Doors were utilized as makeshift table, with tubs underneath to catch the blood.

In 1861, Thomas J. Abel of the 4th Iowa Cavalry served in Springfield, Missouri. In 1863, Abel became captain of the 56th US Colored Infantry in Helena, Arkansas, following the battle on July 4, 1863. Abel had this photograph of the Union's General Hospital—the house with columns—saved in an album. "Southern burying ground along ridge & back in woods beyond hospital" is written on the back.

In 1860, 29-year-old Maine native Aurelius T. Bartlett traveled from Illinois to the gold rush at Colorado's Pike's Peak. Upon his return, he became surgeon for the 33rd Missouri Infantry, at Benton Barracks in St. Louis. Bartlett tended the wounded while the infantry pursued Gen. Sterling Price throughout Arkansas and Missouri, chased Gen. John B. Hood in Tennessee, and fought the Battle of Helena on July 4, 1863.

The German-born Dr. John Becker, of Iowa Point, Kansas, poses here with his wife, Margaret "Maggie" Blackburn Becker. Becker was commissioned as assistant surgeon for the 13th Kansas Infantry and mustered in at Camp Stanton, in Atchison, Kansas, in September 1862. In December 1862, Becker was kept busy following the Battle of Prairie Grove, Arkansas, where the 13th Kansas Infantry had suffered heavy casualties.

In 1863, Ela Lawrence Bliss graduated from Chicago's Rush Medical College at 24 years old and became an assistant surgeon in the US Army of the Potomac. In 1865, Bliss (far right) served at several Washington, DC, hospitals, including Lincoln, Georgetown Seminary, and Finley. Discharged and suffering from typhoid fever, Bliss died in the arms of his sister Emma Brainerd Bliss at the home of their uncle C.H. Hurd, in New Rochelle, New York, on August 23, 1865, while traveling home.

Benjamin Seymour Goodyear was the oldest of four sons of Elizabeth and Timothy Goodyear, a carriage maker from Macon, Georgia. Benjamin enlisted as a private at age 15 in May 1862. Initially appointed a musician, he became a hospital steward at General Hospital No. 8, otherwise known as St. Charles Hospital, in Richmond, Virginia. He was present during the Confederate surrender at Appomattox, Virginia, on April 9, 1865.

Graduating from the New York University School of Medicine in 1857, James Lawlor Kiernan, 20, edited New York's *Medical Press*. He became assistant surgeon for the 69th New York State Militia and was named surgeon to the 6th Missouri Cavalry in 1862. At Port Gibson, Mississippi, Kiernan was captured and wounded. President Lincoln appointed Kiernan brigadier general of volunteers in 1863. After the war, Kiernan became US Pension Bureau surgeon and consul to China.

In 1865, Chaplain Paul Wald served at the officer's hospital in Natchez, Mississippi. According to historian Thomas P. Lowry, Wald was convicted of being drunk on duty, encouraging coworkers to visit prostitutes, and threatening to kill a hospital steward. He was discharged on April 8, 1865, and later taught German at the O'Fallon School in St. Louis. Wald died in 1886, orphaning his son, Emile, 17, and daughter, Rosa, 15.

In 1861, Capt. Augustus H. Kilty organized a naval flotilla in St. Louis, where he commanded the 512-ton, ironclad screw steamer USS *Mound City*, named for the Illinois city where it was built by James B. Eads. While attacking Fort St. Charles, Arkansas, in 1862, *Mound City*'s steam-drum boiler was shot. Escaping steam killed nearly 100 men and scalded Kilty's left hand, requiring its amputation. Meanwhile, 40 men were shot or drowned attempting to escape. *Mound City* is seen here in 1864.

Pennsylvania native Hiram Simons Leffingwell graduated from St. Louis Medical College in 1863. He became surgeon for the 65th US Colored Infantry at Benton Barracks. The infantry served garrison duty at Morganza, Baton Rouge, and Port Hudson, Louisiana, until 1867. In 1869, Leffingwell, 32, married Elma C. Cornell, 24, of Virginia, and moved his medical practice to Wisconsin. In 1903, he began receiving a $30 monthly pension for his military service.

William Thomson was the assistant surgeon for the 198th Pennsylvania Infantry, Gen. George B. McClellan's medical director, and the supervisor of Douglas Hospital in Washington, DC. He also received a commendation from President Lincoln for his leadership as a field surgeon and pioneered the use of photography to record wound appearances and pathological conditions. He also made contributions to the Army Medical Museum and the field of ophthamology, especially in the area of color blindness.

William W. Bailey, born in the Indian Territory in 1839, became surgeon for the 1st Missouri Cavalry at Jefferson Barracks in St. Louis in September 1861. The 1st Missouri Cavalry joined Gen. John C. Fremont in Springfield for his 1861 Missouri Campaign. In 1862 and 1863, the men fought rebels and guerrillas. For most of 1865, Bailey and some of the 1st Missouri Cavalry were stationed at Fort Smith, Arkansas.

In 1862, Missouri governor Hamilton R. Gamble appointed David V. Whitney, 21, assistant surgeon of the 4th Missouri State Militia Cavalry. The cavalry fought in the Second Battle of Springfield on January 8, 1863, while Whitney supervised Springfield's Central General Hospital. In 1863, he became an assistant surgeon in the Navy. After the war, Whitney traveled west, where he visited Missouri River Indian tribes and became a prospector and deputy US marshal.

Ambulances, initially under the command of the Quartermaster's Corps, were a rare commodity, and officers frequently confiscated them for their own personal use. Field care fell to assistant surgeons who relied on stretcher-bearers to transport the wounded. Initially, single horse–drawn two-wheeled ambulances were typical. This ambulance was dispatched to the Bull Run battlefield in northern Virginia on July 22, 1861. Dr. Jonathan Letterman created the first Ambulance Corps in 1862.

When Kansas joined the Union on January 29, 1861, a star was added to the US flag. President Lincoln refused to acknowledge the southern states' rights to secede by allowing any stars to be removed from the flag. The new 34-star US flag, like the two-story flag hanging from this St. Louis hospital, continued to be used until July 3, 1863, when another star was added to the flag for West Virginia.

Dr. Joseph P. Root was chairman of the Free-State Executive Committee. He located the road from Nebraska City, Nebraska, to Topeka, Kansas, securing safe travel for free-state immigrants. In 1861, Root became the first lieutenant governor of Kansas. He also served as 2nd Kansas Cavalry surgeon and Army of the Frontier medical director from 1862 through 1865. In 1870, Root was appointed minister to Chile. He passed away in Wyandotte, Kansas, in 1885.

Born in Ohio, Myron W. Robbins, 25, graduated from Rush Medical College in Chicago in 1854. Major Robbins, brother-in-law of Gen. Grenville Dodge, became the 4th Iowa Infantry surgeon in July 1861. In 1879, Robbins relocated to Las Vegas, where he co-founded the New Mexico Medical Society, earning $200 per year as a physician. In 1903, Robbins died at the National Home for Disabled Volunteer Soldiers in Leavenworth, Kansas.

In 1861, Virginia became a Confederate state, but Fort Monroe, known as "Fortress Freedom," remained in Union hands. A 1,800-bed military hospital, which had a high mortality rate despite being well staffed, was established there. In 1862, Fort Monroe began burying its deceased soldiers at Hampton National Cemetery. The largest moat-encircled masonry fortification in the United States, Fort Monroe was formally deactivated by the US Army on September 15, 2011.

Hospital stewards, such as this unidentified Union soldier, were selected by the regimental surgeon from the unit's enlisted men. As noncommissioned officers receiving the same pay as a sergeant major, hospital stewards were the lowest-ranking members of both the Union and Confederate medical departments. Army regulation qualifications included honesty, reliability, intelligence, and temperance, because they dispensed medicinal whiskey and prescription drugs. They also had to be literate in order to keep records.

In September 1862, Jeffrey R. Thomas, 35, became assistant surgeon in the 112th New York Infantry. Just three months later, Thomas was discharged at Suffolk, Virginia, for a physical disability he received at the Battle at Deserted Farms, Virginia. Several men in the regiment died from typhoid fever during garrison duty in Suffolk. Following his discharge, Thomas opened a medical practice in Bay City, Michigan, and died of pneumonia in 1883.

USS *Red Rover*, shown beside an ice barge during the war, was built at Cape Girardeau, Missouri, in 1859. In 1861, the Confederate Navy used this 625-ton side-wheel steamer until its capture at Island No. 10, Missouri, in April 1862. She became the US Navy's first hospital ship, with the Catholic order Sisters of the Holy Cross serving on *Red Rover* as the first female nurses aboard ship.

This unidentified soldier was photographed while recuperating from an amputation. As amputees came home from the war, artificial limbs, known as prosthetics, became a necessity. In 1866, North Carolina became the first state to offer Confederate veterans an artificial limb or, in lieu of a prosthetic, $70 for a leg or $50 for an arm. Over 1,500 inquired about prosthetics, but most took the money. The state program, which ended in 1870, cost over $81,000.

In 1854, Abel Cummings Roberts earned his medical degree at the University of Michigan. In 1859, Dr. Roberts moved to Fort Madison, Iowa, where he practiced medicine and became owner/editor of the *Fort Madison Democrat*. In 1863, Dr. Roberts became the 21st Missouri Infantry surgeon, a post he held through 1866. Major Roberts operated for 48 hours straight during serious engagements, often by candlelight. He claimed that no man died on his "operating table," which was often just the ground.

Five

Bushwhackers, Guerrillas, Jayhawkers, and Other Nefarious Characters

During the fall of 1862 and the winter of 1863, guerrilla John S. Nichols (shown here) frustrated Union authorities by robbing travelers and remote homesteads throughout northwest Missouri. When he was captured in April 1863, Nichols proclaimed his innocence but admitted serving in the Missouri State Guard under Gen. Sterling Price. As proof that he was occupied elsewhere, Nichols testified that he participated in the battles at Pea Ridge, Arkansas, in March 1862 and Lone Jack, Missouri, in August 1862, as well as the Second Battle of Springfield in January 1863. Nichols was tried, found guilty, and sentenced to hanging. On October 30, 1863, at 3:00 p.m., approximately 1,500 men, women, and children stood on a rise outside of Jefferson City, Missouri, to watch the first "rebel" hung by the Union authorities in Missouri. Nichol's sister, Martha, kissed him goodbye before he ascended the gallows steps. As the rope was placed around his neck, he stated, "Gentlemen, I am going to show you how a Confederate soldier dies."

James Henry "Jim" Lane was a lawyer, Kansas senator, and soldier who served under 12th US president Zachary Taylor during the Mexican War. General Lane led the "Kansas Brigade," becoming a ruthless Jayhawker leader. Lane faced off against Confederate general Sterling Price during the Battle of Dry Wood Creek, Missouri, on September 2, 1861, and then three weeks later plundered and burned Osceola, Missouri. In 1863, William Clarke Quantrill retaliated with the Lawrence, Kansas, massacre. Lane committed suicide in 1866.

At age 20, William Clarke Quantrill, alias Charley Hart, relocated from Ohio to Kansas, becoming an infamous secessionist guerrilla. Quantrill became captain of the Confederate regiment Quantrill's Company, Missouri. Quantrill led 450 of his partisan raiders during the massacre of 200 citizens and the burning of Lawrence, Kansas, on August 21, 1863. On June 6, 1865, Union troops killed Quantrill in a surprise raid in Louisville, Kentucky.

James Gilpatrick Blunt went to sea as a teenager, became a physician, and helped draft the Kansas constitution. During the Civil War, he was appointed brigadier general of volunteers for the Department of Kansas. In 1862, during the Battle of Prairie Grove, Arkansas, Blunt repulsed Gen. Thomas C. Hindman's Confederate advance into Missouri. Blunt commanded the first "colored" regiments and several Native American regiments. On October 6, 1863, Blunt and his bodyguard of 75 men were surprised near Baxter Springs, Kansas, by William C. Quantrill and about 650 guerrillas disguised as Union soldiers and flying a Union flag. Quantrill set an example for his band of partisan raiders by killing a disarmed wounded man. The 9th Wisconsin Cavalry brigade band had 14 members killed and burned in their bandwagon. General Blunt escaped with a handful of men.

Maj. Henry Zarah Curtis, son of Brig. Gen. Samuel R. Curtis, commander of southwest Missouri, was Gen. James G. Blunt's adjutant general when Confederate guerrilla William C. Quantrill attacked Union soldiers at Baxter Springs, Kansas, in October 1863. Major Curtis fell from his horse and was taken prisoner and shot. General Curtis named Fort Zarah, Kansas, in his son's honor. Henry's funeral was one of the largest ever held in Keokuk, Iowa.

William Thomason Anderson, seen here in a postmortem photograph, participated with William C. Quantrill's Confederate guerrilla raiders. Dubbed "Bloody Bill" Anderson, he attacked Federal troops and Unionist citizens, cutting off his victim's ears, noses, and scalps, which he then displayed from his bridle. In August 1863, Anderson participated in the massacre at Lawrence, Kansas. A year later, Anderson and his band of bushwhackers shot, scalped, disemboweled, and beheaded over 170 Union soldiers in Centralia, Missouri.

Isaac J. "Ike" Hall and three of his brothers joined William C. Quantrill after Kansas Jayhawkers burned their Cass County, Missouri, home. After following Quantrill to Kentucky, the gang was ambushed and Quantrill was captured on May 10, 1865. Isaac escaped by hiding in a pond. He and Quantrill's surviving gang members surrendered in July 1865, at Samuel's Depot in Nelson County, Kentucky. Ike, Robert, and John Hall were paroled and decided to settle in Kentucky.

Born in 1843 in Centralia, Missouri, Clark L. Hockensmith was killed attempting to save Confederate guerrilla William C. Quantrill on May 10, 1865, in Kentucky. Why Hockensmith joined the guerrillas is unknown, but even as a child, he was described by those who knew him as loyal, brave, and generous. Quantrill's deathbed request was to "have Clark Hockensmith buried like a soldier." Hockensmith is buried at Maple Grove Cemetery, Bloomfield, Kentucky.

Kentuckian John G. Jarrett (Jarrette) holds an 1851 Colt. He and his brother-in-law, Cole Younger, joined Confederate guerrilla William C. Quantrill in 1861. In the late 1860s, Jarrett participated with Jesse James in a bank robbery in Russellville, Kentucky, as well as several in Missouri. In 1868, vigilantes reportedly shot Jarrett and his wife, Mary Jospehine "Josie," before burning their house with their two children—Jephtha Younger Jarrett, 6, and Margaret, 4—inside. The children reportedly survived.

Born in 1852, Missourian James Andrew "Dick" Liddil (Liddell) became a horse thief, train robber, and killer. He rode with William C. Quantrill during the war, and after the war, he rode with Jesse and Frank James. He co-owned the Bank Saloon with Bob Ford in Las Vegas in 1880. Then, in 1882, Ford killed Jesse James, and Liddil turned state's evidence against the James Gang. He died in 1901, in Covington, Kentucky.

George Webster Maddox was born in Missouri in 1831. George and his brother, Richard, joined William C. Quantrill's Confederate guerrillas in January 1862. Maddox participated in the raids at Pleasant Hill, Missouri, in 1862, Lawrence and Baxter Springs, Kansas, in 1863, and Centralia, Missouri, in 1864. Maddox was the only guerrilla to stand trial for the atrocities committed at Lawrence. Eventually, he worked as a guard at the Missouri State Penitentiary in 1887.

In February 1861, David A. Alexander, 22, deputy city clerk of Napoleon, Arkansas, joined the "Napoleon Cavalry" 6th High Arkansas Militia. When Arkansas seceded, Alexander became a second lieutenant in the 1st Arkansas Mounted Rifles. Within a month, two murders occurred within his company. At Fort Smith, Arkansas, Alexander stabbed Pvt. William Finnerty to death, and Pvt. LeRoy Weatherford killed Cpl. John Tinney. Alexander was court-martialed and cashiered at Camp Yancey, Arkansas, while Weatherford was later promoted to lieutenant.

Charles Fletcher "Fletch" Taylor participated with William C. Quantrill's Missouri Partisan Raiders in the massacre at Lawrence, Kansas, in 1863 and earned a $10,000 price on his head. In 1864, his left arm was amputated after being shot. Following the war, Fletch ran with the James Gang and the Younger Brothers, and reportedly participated in the Liberty, Missouri, bank robbery in 1866. Fletch is seen here with his wife, Isabella, in Alabama after their 1878 wedding in Joplin, Missouri.

In 1855, Dr. Rueben Samuel became stepfather to Alexander Franklin and Jesse Woodson when he married their twice widowed mother, Zerelda James Simms. Dr. Samuel gave up medicine to sell slaves and farm. Union soldiers tortured him while seeking information regarding the guerrilla activities of the boys, better known as Frank and Jesse James. Their mother supported their activities, naming their half sister Fannie Quantrill Samuel after their gang leader, William C. Quantrill.

Isaac "Ike" Berry (left) and his brothers, Sam "One-Armed" and Richard Berry, joined Marcellus Jerome Clarke (right) when William C. Quantrill moved his remaining band of guerrillas to Kentucky in 1864. Clarke, dubbed "Sue Mundy," due to his long hair and feminine features, was hanged on March 15, 1865. After the war, Ike and Richard Berry went with Gen. Joseph O. Shelby on the famous expedition to relocate Confederates to Mexico.

Following the brutal murders of his wife and child by Missouri guerrillas in 1857, Dr. Charles Ransford Jennison supported and participated in the campaigns of the abolitionist John Brown. During the war, Colonel Jennison and the 7th Kansas Cavalry, dubbed "Jennison's Jayhawkers," patrolled the borders of Kansas. After the war, Jennison and his second wife, Mary, lived in Leavenworth, Kansas, and Jennison became a two-term Kansas state representative and a Kansas senator in 1871.

The building below, now called John Brown's Fort, began as the armory's fire engine and guardhouse in Harper's Ferry, Virginia, in 1848. After 1855, abolitionist Brown and his five sons justified murdering proslavery Kansas settlers by claiming it was "the will of a just God." In October 1859, Brown and 21 followers, including three of his sons—Oliver, Owen, and Watson, barricaded themselves in the "fort," attempting to provoke a black rebellion. Col. Robert E. Lee's militia squelched the revolt. Brown was wounded, but ten followers, including Oliver and Watson, were killed. Brown was hanged on December 2, 1859. In 1891, the fort was moved for display near the Chicago World's Columbian Exposition, which opened in 1893. In 1909, which was the 50th anniversary of John Brown's raid, Storer College, one of the first black colleges, purchased John Brown's Fort. It was acquired in 1960 by the National Park Service.

Six

Minorities Serving the Causes

Born near Rome, Georgia, in 1806, Isaac "Stand" Watie was named De'gata'ga, loosely translated into "Stand." In 1836, Watie and his brother, Elias Boudinot, signed Pres. Andrew Jackson's Treaty of New Echota, which led to the infamous Trail of Tears march, during which approximately 4,000 Native Americans perished. In 1861, Colonel Watie raised the 1st Cherokee Mounted Rifles and was chief of the Confederate Cherokees from 1862 to 1865. Watie's poorly equipped troops fought in more than 25 major engagements and several skirmishes. Their greatest conquests occurred in 1864, when they captured the Federal steamboat *J.R. Williams*, worth over $100,000, and during the Second Battle of Cabin Creek, Oklahoma, when they seized $1.5 million in Union supplies. In May 1864, Watie became the only Native American brigadier general for the Confederacy, and in June 1865 he was the last Confederate general to surrender. In 1866, Watie and his son Saladin Watie, 19, went to Washington, DC, with the Southern Cherokee delegation to negotiate a reconstruction treaty. Watie died in 1871 and was commemorated with a US Civil War Series stamp in 1995.

Samuel H. Gunter was born in 1840 in Skin-Bayou District, Cherokee Nation, in what is now Oklahoma. Shown here wearing a "hunting coat," Gunter joined the Confederate 1st Cherokee Mounted Rifles Indian Cavalry Division in 1861, and he became one of Col. Stand Watie's most daring men. In 1864, Gunter married Fannie Daniel of the Choctaw Nation, and he became assistant chief of the Cherokee Nation in 1871, dying two years later.

Around 1850, the American Indian Association ordained Daniel N. McIntosh a Baptist preacher. McIntosh was the nephew of Rolly McIntosh, "King of the Creeks." In 1861, Daniel signed the Creek Treaty of Alliance with the Confederate States of America and organized the 1st Creek Mounted Volunteers, which became part of the 1st Indian Cavalry Brigade under Gen. Stand Watie. McIntosh County, Oklahoma, was named for his family.

In 1839, at age 10, Oliver Hazard "Perry" Brewer (seen here later in life) walked with five-year-old Delia Amelia Vann at Sawyer's School for Girls in Fayetteville, Arkansas. In 1854, Brewer married Delia, the daughter of "Rich Joe" Vann, a wealthy Cherokee businessman. A slave owner in 1860, Brewer became a first lieutenant in Stand Watie's 2nd Cherokee Mounted Rifles. After the war, he served as the president of the Cherokee Board of Education and on the Cherokee Nation's supreme court.

Lt. Col. Clement Neely Vann fought with the 1st Cherokee Mounted Rifles from 1861 to 1866. In November 1870, Vann became treasurer of the Cherokee Nation, earning $500 per year. In 1871, Vann and former Confederate Cherokee William Penn Adair formed the Texas Cherokees and Associated Bands (TCAB). Through lawsuits, the TCAB attempted to regain 1.5 million acres from the Republic of Texas that the 1836 Treaty of Bowles Village had granted them.

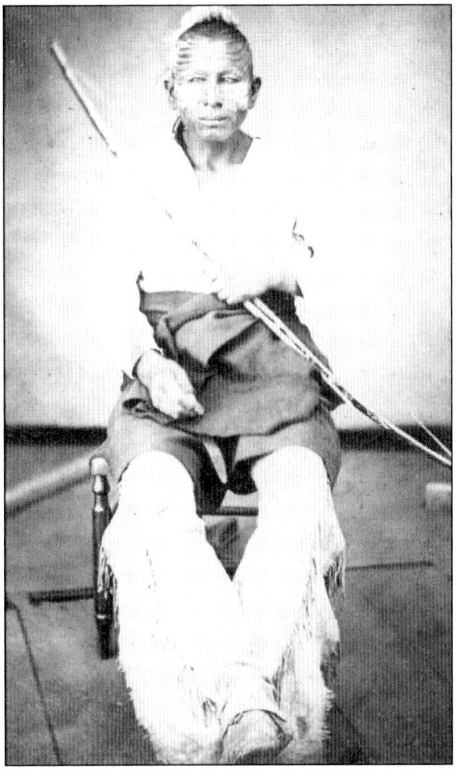

During the Civil War, the Greater Osage tribe became Confederates, while the Little Osage were Federals. Organized in 1863, the 1st Osage Battalion, commanded by Maj. Broken Arm, was assigned to Gen. Douglas H. Cooper and Col. Stand Watie's Trans-Mississippi Department brigade. After the war, the US government took most of the Osages' Kansas land as punishment for the Greater Osage's Confederate affiliation. An unidentified Osage warrior is seen at left.

William Penn Adair was a soldier, a lawyer, and a friend of Pres. Ulysses S. Grant. He was also the leader and representative from the Cherokee Nation to Washington, DC, from 1866 until his death in 1880. Colonel Adair, of the 2nd Cherokee Mounted Volunteers, served with Clem V. Rogers, the father of Adair's namesake, William Penn Adair Rogers, better known as comedian and humorist Will Rogers. Adair County, Oklahoma, was named in honor of the Adair family.

In 1833, William Lloyd Garrison founded the American Anti-Slavery Society, which also supported women's suffrage. By 1840, women such as Susan B. Anthony and Amelia Bloomer were among its 250,000 members. This 1851 *Liberty Almanac* was published in New York by the American and Foreign Anti-Slavery Society, which had formed as a rival organization in 1840. The publication is similar to today's *Farmer's Almanac*, except the articles advocate abolishing slavery. Unfortunately, the American and Foreign Anti-Slavery Society did not support women's suffrage.

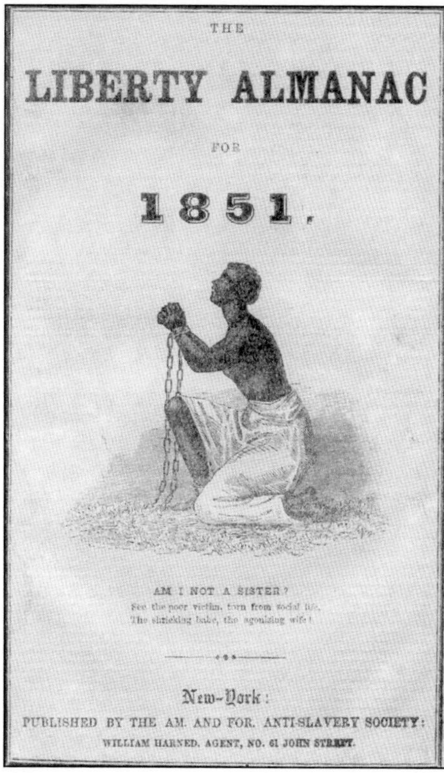
THE

LIBERTY ALMANAC

FOR

1851.

AM I NOT A SISTER?

See the poor victim, torn from social life,
The shrieking babe, the agonizing wife!

New-York:

PUBLISHED BY THE AM. AND FOR. ANTI-SLAVERY SOCIETY:

WILLIAM HARNED, AGENT, NO. 61 JOHN STREET.

In 1862, Harrison DuBois, 30, fought at Prairie Grove, Arkansas, in the 11th Kansas Cavalry. In 1864, he became captain of the 62nd US Colored Infantry, stationed in Morganza, Louisiana, and Brazo-Santiago Island, Texas. More than a month after Gen. Robert E. Lee surrendered in Virginia, 250 of the 62nd US Colored Infantrymen fought the last Civil War battle at Palmetto Ranch, Texas, on May 12–13, 1865.

African American soldiers such as this unidentified US Colored Troops infantryman proved themselves as fighters but struggled for equal pay. They earned $7 per month plus a $3 clothing allowance, while white soldiers received $13 per month without clothing subtractions. In the Confederate Army, the free black soldiers, cooks, musicians, and teamsters earned the same pay as their white counterparts. Congress granted black soldiers equal pay on June 15, 1864.

When the 1st Kansas Colored Volunteer Infantry fought at Island Mound, Missouri, on October 29, 1862, Missouri became the first state with African Americans, like this US Colored Troops infantryman, fighting in battle. By 1862, President Lincoln approved congressional bills creating Army and Navy Medals of Honor to reward "gallantry in action." Since, there have been 37 black Civil War soldiers and sailors awarded the Medal of Honor.

On September 22, 1862, Pres. Abraham Lincoln issued the preliminary Emancipation Proclamation promising freedom to Confederate state slaves if those states did not return to the Union by January 1, 1863. The Union Army quickly recruited African Americans, gaining approximately 179,000 men, and organized them into 166 regiments, creating about a 10-percent increase in the size of the Union Army. Another 19,000 African Americans served in the US Navy. More than 80 percent of those recruited were former Confederate state slaves. On January 1, 186, Lincoln issued the final Emancipation Proclamation, granting freedom to slaves in the Confederate states.

This unidentified US Colored Troop soldier is representative of the freemen and loyal Unionist slaves who formed Missouri's first black regiment, the 3rd Arkansas Infantry (African Descent) in 1863. They organized at Schofield Barracks in St. Louis, becoming the 56th US Colored Infantry in 1864. They served garrison duty in Helena, Arkansas, until 1866. The 56th USCI lost 43 percent of its men, with only 25 dying in battle and 649 dying from disease.

In 1863, 1st Sgt. William "August" Messley joined the 1st Missouri Infantry (African Descent), in St. Louis, where he contracted acute rheumatic disease. First Sergeant Messley is seen here in Glasgow, Missouri, in 1864, when the infantry became the 62nd US Colored Infantry. Messley's rheumatic pains were aggravated by sleeping in a "fly tent" in Port Hudson, Louisiana. In 1865, he fought during the war's last battle at Palmetto Ranch in Brownsville, Texas.

Both Union and Confederate women, black and white, assisted with the war effort through obvious and clandestine actions. They offered tremendous assistance to military forces and their operations. Black women like escaped slave Harriet Tubman, the Underground Railroad "Conductor," and this unidentified woman acted as couriers, spies, scouts, and nurses. In June 1863, Tubman helped Col. James Montgomery and 300 black Union soldiers of the 2nd South Carolina Infantry (African Descent) liberate 800 slaves on the Combahee River in South Carolina.

Born in Louisiana, Robert "Bob" Walker enlisted in 1863 at age 11. His listed occupation was field hand or servant, which probably meant slave. The US Navy enlisted these "contrabands" and classified them as boys or landsmen. Walker became a third-class boy on the ironclad USS *Pittsburgh* until June 1865, after which he joined the side-wheel steamer *Tempest* through September 1865, earning $8 per month. Walker was photographed at Mound City, Illinois, in 1864.

Prominent German-born St. Louis businessman Franz Hassendeubel commanded the 3rd Missouri Infantry, formed almost entirely of Germans. In August 1861, Hassendeubel joined the newly formed 17th Missouri Infantry, which became part of the Army of the Cumberland. The 17th Missouri Infantry was constantly in the field, suffering severe losses of men and officers, including Hassendeubel, who died from wounds received during the Battle of Vicksburg in July 1863.

Hungarian Anselm J. Albert relocated to the US in 1850 after serving in the Austro-Hungarian Army during 1848–1849. Albert helped organize the Missouri Home Guard and captured Camp Jackson in St. Louis in May 1861. Afterwards, Albert became lieutenant colonel in Col. Franz Sigel's predominantly German 3rd Missouri Infantry. Wounded during the Wilson's Creek battle in August 1861, Albert later became Gen. John C. Fremont's chief of staff.

In 1847, 11-year-old German Frederick William Schaurte became a sailor. In 1854, he sailed aboard *Tropic* into New York City and joined the 2nd US Infantry. In 1861, First Lieutenant Schaurte reenlisted in the 6th Kansas Cavalry and a year later, he was commissioned by President Lincoln as Lt. Col. Schaurte of the 2nd Cherokee Indian Brigade, which fought the largest battle in the Indian Territory, at Honey Springs, Oklahoma, in July 1863.

German immigrant Dr. Bernard Bruns, 61, was the surgeon of the 42nd Enrolled Missouri Militia. His son, Capt. Heinrich "Henry" G. Bruns, 19, of the 10th Missouri Cavalry, became Jefferson City's first Civil War casualty, at Iuka, Mississippi, in 1863. The next year, Bernard passed away. His widow, Henriette, turned their house, which was across the street from the state capitol, into a boardinghouse for politicians and antislavery Unionist organizations like the "Radical Unionists."

In 1851, Leo Rassieur immigrated from Wadern, Prussia, following his mother's death. At age 17, Rassieur enlisted in the 1st US Regular Company. He became ill while serving as post adjutant at Warsaw, Missouri, and was discharged in April 1862. Upon recovering in October, Rassieur became captain and drillmaster of the 34th Missouri Infantry at Benton Barracks in St. Louis. The 34th Missouri was renamed the 30th Missouri Infantry and dubbed the "Shamrock Regiment."

Egbert Benson Brown was the original lieutenant colonel of the 7th Missouri Infantry, called the "Irish 7th" because of its high percentage of Irish enlistees. In 1861, the infantry joined Gen. John C. Fremont's Springfield Campaign after organizing in St. Louis. In 1863, the men joined Grant's Army of the Tennessee. The regiment carried a painted green silk standard, decorated with an Irish harp, shamrocks, and an American eagle.

In May 1861, Bernard Gaines Farrar Jr. became aide-de-camp to Gen. Nathaniel Lyon. Following Lyon's death during the Battle of Wilson's Creek in August, Farrar organized the 30th Missouri Infantry, known as the Shamrock Regiment. In 1862, Farrar organized a black regiment in Natchez, Mississippi, called the 6th US Colored Heavy Artillery. In 1864, the 7th Missouri Veterans Infantry consolidated with the 30th Missouri Infantry, becoming known as the "Missouri Irish Battalion."

Seven

Boys in Blue and Other Union Supporters

Named for his paternal grandfather, Abraham Lincoln was known for his unwavering honesty. As a young man, he excelled at stump speaking, wrestling, and storytelling. At age 17, Lincoln earned 37¢ per day assisting ferryboats across the Ohio River in Illinois. During the Black Hawk War in 1831–1832, Lincoln became captain of the 4th Illinois Volunteers, for which he received a 160-acre land grant in Springfield, Illinois. Never a demonstrative man, Lincoln was still sensitive and romantic. He wrote the song sung at the 1826 wedding of his sister, Sarah. In 1833, Lincoln lived in James Rutledge's tavern. Rutledge, the founder of Salem, Illinois, was the father of Anne Rutledge, the love of Lincoln's life. In 1835, they became engaged, but Anne soon died. Following rejections from two women, Lincoln finally became engaged to Mary Todd in 1840, but left her standing at the altar on January 1, 1841. They finally wed almost two years later on November 4, 1842. Mary was beside Lincoln when he was shot by John Wilkes Booth at Ford's Theatre in Washington, DC, on April 14, 1865.

When Tennessee seceded, Sen. Andrew Johnson remained in the US Senate. President Lincoln rewarded Johnson's Union loyalty by appointing him military governor of Tennessee, which led to his nomination for vice president, during Lincoln's 1864 presidential campaign. Following Lincoln's assassination on April 14, 1865, Johnson became the 17th president. During his administration, Alaska was purchased and Nebraska became the 37th state. Nebraska's capital at the time was Lancaster, but it was renamed Lincoln in honor of the president.

In 1860, Edwin McMasters Stanton left a prospering law practice to become Pres. James Buchanan's attorney general. The next year, Stanton became a legal advisor to President Lincoln's secretary of war, Simon Cameron, and replaced him in 1862. As head of internal security, many blamed Stanton for Lincoln's assassination. Beside Lincoln's deathbed, Stanton stated this famous phrase as Lincoln died: "Now he belongs to the ages." Many believe he said "angels" instead of "ages."

The famous midget Gen. Tom Thumb was made famous by Phineas "P.T." Barnum. In 1842, Barnum met the 25-inch-tall Charles Sherwood Stratton when Stratton was only four years old and trained him to perform in his New York City American Museum. In 1863, Thumb married 32-inch-tall Lavinia Warren, "The Little Queen of Beauty," in front of 2,000 guests. Civil War photographer Matthew Brady photographed the newlyweds, who visited President Lincoln at the White House on their honeymoon.

In 1864, newspapers reported that Mrs. Francis L Clayton, disguised as a man, enlisted with her husband during 1861, in St. Paul, Minnesota. Clayton claimed she fought 18 battles beside her husband, was taken prisoner once, and was wounded in her hand, knee, and hip. Clayton divulged her sex to her general when her husband was killed during the Battle of Stones River, in Murfreesboro, Tennessee, in 1862. She was immediately discharged.

Christopher Houston "Kit" Carson was a trapper, scout, Indian agent, and folk hero of Western dime novels and films. In 1842, Carson guided Lt. John C. Fremont to California. In 1861, 51-year-old Carson became colonel of the 1st New Mexico Infantry. In 1864, Carson relocated 8,000 Navajo on the Long Walk, a 300-mile forced march, and later fought his last battle at Adobe Walls, Texas. He retired in 1867 as a lieutenant colonel and died within a year. The capital of Nevada, Carson City, is named in his honor.

Following his graduation from West Point in 1830, Meriwether Lewis Clark, son of William Clark, of the famed Lewis and Clark Expedition, served during the Black Hawk War. He eventually became a St. Louis architect and designed the town's first theater, the St. Louis Theatre, in 1837, as well as the St. Vincent de Paul Church, in 1845. Clark served in the Missouri State Guard and as colonel of artillery under Gen. Braxton Bragg.

In 1861, nine-year-old runaway John Lincoln Clem served with the 22nd Michigan Infantry. He officially enlisted in 1863 and was dubbed the "Drummer Boy of Chickamauga," but Pres. Ulysses S. Grant commissioned Clem a second lieutenant. When he retired in 1916, Major General Clem was the last active-duty Civil War veteran. In 1941, the USS *Santa Ana* was renamed USAT *John L. Clem*. Clem's hometown of Newark, Ohio, named General John Lincoln Clem Elementary School in his honor.

To enlist in either the Union or Confederate Army, a man had to be at least 18 years old. After February 1864, the Confederates lowered their age requirement to 17. However, boys of only 13 were drummer boys, musicians, errand boys, and shoe-shiners. This unidentified child is dressed in the distinctive jacket and baggy trousers of the Zouave-style uniform, which resembled the uniforms of the original Zouaves of the French Army.

Thomas Hart Benton was a five-term US senator, a lawyer, and the editor of the *Missouri Enquirer.* In the 1820s, Benton opposed Missouri's slavery restrictions, but in 1835, he emancipated Sarah, a 41-year-old slave who had belonged to the family of his wife, Elizabeth, since birth. Benton advocated westward expansion, and his son-in-law, Gen. John C. Fremont, secured the US claim to the Oregon Territory. In 1847, Benton County, Oregon, was named in Benton's honor.

George Caleb Bingham was a self-taught artist, a respected politician, and a Civil War captain from Van Horn's Battalion, which fought at Lexington, Missouri. After the war, Captain Bingham served on the school board of Independence, Missouri, and was the police commissioner of Kansas City, Missouri. As Missouri's adjutant general, Bingham exposed the Ku Klux Klan movement in southwest Missouri. Bingham's second wife, Mattie, founded the Confederate Widows and Orphans Home in Kansas City.

Benjamin Gratz Brown was a lawyer, state and national politician, and editor of the *Missouri Democrat*. In 1856, "Gratz" Brown was shot in the knee while dueling with future lieutenant governor Thomas C. Reynolds over Reynolds's slanderous remarks in a rival newspaper regarding Brown's antislavery sentiments. In 1861, Colonel Brown organized the 4th US Reserve Corps, which reinforced Gen. Franz Siegel in Carthage, Missouri. In 1872, Brown built the Missouri Governor's Mansion, in Jefferson City.

B.Gratz Brown.

In 1861, Benjamin Franklin "Frank" Paramore lied to join the 57th Indiana Infantry at the age of 14. His brother, Jesse Webster Paramore, joined the 9th Minnesota Infantry in 1862. In 1864, Jesse was promoted to the 65th US Colored Infantry, which lost 34 percent of its regiment. A third brother, Marquis De Lafayette "Lafe" Paramore, served with the 16th Indiana and the 72nd Illinois Infantry, while a fourth brother, George Washington Paramore, joined the 8th Indiana Infantry.

In 1862, Lt. Harrison A. "Harry" Gleim joined the 2nd Missouri Light Artillery in St. Louis. Lieutenant Gleim became aide-de-camp to Gen. John Schofield and Brig. Gen. Lewis Merrill. In 1869, Gleim's brothers, Frailey and John, purchased Rose Hill Seminary, later the Gleim Mansion, in Tipton, Missouri. During the war, it was Gen. John C. Fremont's Union Army headquarters. Harrison began Tipton's Grand Army of the Republic (GAR) Post No. 512.

Minister and renowned orator Henry Ward Beecher, the brother of novelist Harriet Beecher Stowe, supplied rifles, known as "Beecher's Bibles" to abolitionist John Brown in 1856. During the war, President Lincoln sent Beecher to London to persuade Great Britain to remain neutral. On April 14, 1865, the day Lincoln was assassinated, Beecher gave the sermon during Fort Sumter's "Raising of the Flag" ceremony.

Arrested for leading the 1857 Kansas Constitutional Convention banning slavery, George Washington Deitzler later became speaker of the Kansas House of Representatives and mayor of Lawrence, Kansas. In 1861, Colonel Deitzler became an agent for the Pottawatomie Indians and served under Gen. Nathaniel Lyon at Wilson's Creek with the 1st Kansas Infantry. In 1862, he served under Gen. Ulysses S. Grant at Vicksburg, and he led the Kansas Militia against Gen. Sterling Price in 1864.

Distinguished Union cavalry leader Gen. Philip Henry Sheridan served as chief quartermaster of the Army of Southwest Missouri. Between 1900 and 1973, General Sheridan was nominated 12 times to the Hall of Fame for Great Americans at New York University's University Heights Campus in the Bronx. In 1973, that campus was sold to City University of New York (CUNY), and became home to the Bronx Community College in 1976. In 1920, the Grand Army of the Republic sent 104 letters, representing 103,000 men, nominating Sheridan, but he was never elected. Generals Robert E. Lee and Ulysses S. Grant are two of the 98 busts in the Hall of Fame. Four additional nominees await the creation of their sculptures.

Future 18th president Ulysses S. Grant graduated from West Point with his future brother-in-law and Civil War aide, Frederick T. Dent. During the Battle of Chickamauga in 1863, General Grant's forces defeated the Confederates. Afterwards, Mathew Brady photographed Grant (left) with unidentified officers on Lookout Mountain Summit in Tennessee. Today, a staircase is located to Grant's right leading to Point Park, a highlight of the 3,000-acre Lookout Mountain Battlefield.

Union general William Tecumseh Sherman rides his famous Kentucky racehorse, Lexington, outside Atlanta, Georgia. The 1864 Georgia Campaign and his famous March to the Sea gained him everlasting fame. The world's largest tree, General Sherman, in Sequoia National Park, bears his name, as does the M4 Sherman tank, which served on all fronts during World War II. The US Post Office Department honored Sherman with commemorative stamps in 1893, 1895, and 1937, and following their reorganization as the US Postal Service in 1971, they issued another Sherman stamp in 1995.

The Stoddard brothers—Truman H., Harley LeGrand, and Andrew M.—of Burlingame, Kansas, fought in the Battle of Prairie Grove, Arkansas, after enlisting in the 11th Kansas Cavalry in 1862. Truman, 33, made sergeant, and Harley LeGrand, 18, became farrier. After Indians shot Harley during the Battle of Platte Bridge Station in the Dakota Territory in July 1865, he mustered out in September, with Truman and 19-year-old Andrew (shown here) at Fort Leavenworth, Kansas.

Capt. Charles Bingley McAfee raised 100 men for Union service and later became staff officer in Springfield, Missouri. After the war, McAfee formed a law firm with John S. Phelps, who became Missouri governor in 1876. McAfee became the criminal court judge of Greene County, Missouri. Judge McAfee was one of the organizers of the Greene County National Bank, the Springfield Wagon Company, the Metropolitan Hotel, and the Springfield Traction Company.

In 1861, Alexander R. Banks (left), an attorney from Minneola, and Arthur W. Gunther, a clerk from Lawrence, served together during the first session of the Kansas House of Representatives. Banks became provost marshal of Kansas, and Gunther became sergeant of the 2nd Kansas Infantry. After the war, Banks became a special US Indian agent and then a special examiner for the Pensions Office (1880–1905), while Gunther bottled beer in Wisconsin.

Hamilton Rowan Gamble began as a lawyer and politician in Missouri in 1818. In 1857, he wrote the dissenting opinion, against slavery, in the Dred Scott Supreme Court case. In 1861, Gamble became Missouri's provisional governor when pro-Southern governor Claiborne Fox Jackson was removed. Gamble worked with President Lincoln to keep Missouri in the Union. In 1862, Gamble created the Enrolled Missouri Militia to combat the guerrilla activities on the Kansas-Missouri border.

In 1819, Thomas Black Reed moved from North Carolina to Randolph County, Missouri, as a newborn. Educated at the University of Missouri, he became a lawyer before fighting bushwhackers for three years as captain of the 9th Missouri State Militia Cavalry, beginning in 1862. Reed served as provost marshal of the District of North Missouri and the District of Rolla. He became a Missouri state senator in 1865.

In 1861, 19-year-old Joseph Catt, of Grasshopper Falls, Kansas, died fighting with the 1st Kansas Infantry during the Battle of Wilson's Creek. The next year, his father, 43-year-old William Catt (seen here) joined the 11th Kansas Cavalry in pursuit of William C. Quantrill and his guerrilla gang. William's wife, Emily Jane Roderick Catt, died in 1863; their youngest son, Alfred E. Catt, died two years later, at just 18 years old, fighting with the 11th Kansas Cavalry.

John White Geary was the first mayor of San Francisco, governor of both Kansas and Pennsylvania, and a Union major general. In 1861, Geary organized the 28th Pennsylvania Infantry and his son, William Logan Geary, served as a musician. Geary's other son, Edward Ratchford Geary, was killed in front of him during the Battle of Wauhatchie, Tennessee, in 1863. Geary County, Kansas, Geary Boulevard in San Francisco, and Pennsylvania State University's Geary Hall were all named in honor of the former general and politician.

Ohio lawyer Charles Daniel Drake relocated to St. Louis in 1834 and worked on the Dred Scott case in 1847. A radical abolitionist during the war, Drake became known for the 1865 Missouri State Constitution, which became known as the "Drake Constitution" for its extreme severity, implementing the death penalty for petty theft as well as murder. Drake was a US senator from Missouri from 1867 to 1873.

University of Munich graduate Henry Flad fled Germany for New York City after the German Revolution in 1848. After becoming an important railroad engineer, Flad relocated to Missouri in 1854. When the war began, Colonel Flad served in Bissell's Engineer Regiment of the West, which became the 1st Missouri Engineers in 1864. After the war, Flad was the assistant of James B. Eads, when he built the St. Louis Bridge, now the Eads Bridge, from 1867 to 1874.

In 1861, Col. David Moore led the 1st Northeast Missouri Home Guard during the northernmost Missouri battle, at Athens. Colonel Moore's sons William W. and Eugene P. "Gene" Moore both served in Col. Martin E. Green's poorly armed Missouri State Guardsmen. In February 1862, the 1st and 2nd Northeast Missouri Home Guards consolidated into the 21st Missouri Infantry commanded by Moore. Two months later, Moore lost his right leg at Shiloh, Tennessee.

During the war, Swiss immigrant Col. John Eugene Smith distinguished himself with the 45th Illinois infantry. Afterwards, he commanded the 27th US Infantry before retiring in 1881. After his death in 1897, Smith was buried under a pyramid-shaped headstone at Greenwood Cemetery in Galena, Illinois. The State of Illinois commissioned Chicago sculptor George E. Ganiere to produce a bust of Smith, which was erected at the Vicksburg National Military Park in 1919.

During the Battle of Big Bethel, Virginia, in 1861, Capt. Hugh Judson Kilpatrick of the 5th New York Infantry became the first regular army officer wounded during the war. Dubbed "Kilcavalry" for blatantly disregarding his cavalrymen's lives, Kilpatrick earned a reputation for dishonesty and infidelity, despite being aggressive and fearless in battle. Kilpatrick died in 1881, when he was the American ambassador to Chili. Heiress and blue jeans entrepreneur Gloria Vanderbilt is Kilpatrick's great-granddaughter.

In 1843, 11-year-old George W. Gilson began his journalism career apprenticed in an Ohio printing company. He served in the Mexican War from 1846 to 1848 and then relocated to Missouri two years later. Gilson joined the 8th Enrolled Missouri Militia in 1861 and became captain of the Missouri Republican Guards in 1862. The latter was formed by employees from St. Louis's *Daily Missouri Republican* newspaper. In 1864, Gilson joined the 40th Missouri Infantry, becoming inspector-general of the St. Louis Military District. After the war, Gilson became city editor for the *Globe-Democrat* and *Missouri-Democrat*.

When the Civil War began, there were only 24 US Navy chaplains. This unidentified chaplain was one of the few who served during the conflict. John L. Lenhart, a Methodist minister from Pennsylvania, served on the USS *Cumberland* from 1860 to 1862. While fighting the ironclad CSS *Virginia*—formerly USS *Merrimack*—at Hampton Roads, Virginia, on March 8, 1862, he became the first US Navy chaplain killed in battle.

In 1855, the Drew family settled in Kansas. In 1861, William Young Drew, 27, and Josiah Richard Drew, 25, joined the 2nd Kansas Infantry. This artillery and cavalry regiment fought in the Battle of Wilson's Creek. A month after, the Drews reenlisted with their brothers, George John Drew, 33 (below), and Charles Pate Drew, 19 (left), in the 11th Kansas Cavalry at Burlingame, Kansas. Their youngest brother, Joseph Samuel Drew, 17, attempted to enlist but was sent home. Joseph later became a sutler to the 6th Kansas Cavalry. Charles and George were wounded during the Battle of Prairie Grove, Arkansas, in December 1862. In 1864, President Lincoln appointed Josiah and George to the 18th US Colored Infantry troop in St. Louis. In 1878, George organized Kansas's Osage County Historical Society, and then he became a War Department clerk in Washington, DC, in 1880.

Eight

Boys in Gray and Other Southern Sympathizers

Robert Edward Lee was descended from the only brothers who signed the Declaration of Independence, Richard Henry Lee and Francis Lightfoot Lee. His father, Henry "Light Horse Harry" Lee, was a Revolutionary War hero. During the Mexican War, from 1846 to 1848, Robert E. Lee served under Gen. Winfield Scott, where he was wounded at Chapultepec. Scott tried to keep Lee in the Union Army, but the strength of his family loyalty prevented him from doing it. Lee could not bring himself to bear arms against family members or fellow Virginians. Lee's resignation became official on April 15, 1861, and he joined the Confederacy. In 1802, Virginia's Augusta Academy in Lexington, Virginia, was renamed Washington College for its benefactor, George Washington. Washington's wife, Martha Dandridge Custis Washington, was the great-grandmother of Lee's wife, Mary Anne Randolph Custis Lee. In 1865, Lee, shown here along with a remnant from a blanket he used during the Civil War, became president of Washington College. Washington College was renamed Washington and Lee University following his death in 1870. Robert and Mary's son, George Washington Custis Lee, then became university president.

In June 1835, Jefferson Finis Davis married Sarah Knox Taylor, the daughter of Margaret Mackell Smith Taylor and Zachary Taylor, the 12th president. The newlyweds immediately visited Davis's siblings in Louisiana. Both arrived with malaria, from which Sarah died. She was buried at Locust Grove, which is now a state historic site. Davis remarried 10 years later, and became president of the Confederacy in 1861.

During the Civil War and Reconstruction, cartoonists' witty interpretations of political and military situations, as well as the social lives of those in power, attempted to relieve tensions with humor as well as convey information. This 1865 cartoon postcard depicts former Confederate president Jefferson Davis, disguised as a woman, being captured by the 4th Michigan Cavalry while attempting to escape to Mexico with his wife, Varina.

In 1845, Varina Anne Banks Howell married Jefferson Davis, who was 18 years her senior. Their marriage survived 44 years, up to the former president of the Confederacy's death in 1889. In 1898, Varina donated their Biloxi, Mississippi, retirement home, Beauvoir, to the Sons of Confederate Veterans. Beauvoir, meaning "beautiful view," became a Confederate Soldiers Home for veterans or their widows. Today, Beauvoir houses the Davis Family Museum and the Confederate Museum.

Alexander Hamilton Stephens picked cotton as a child on the family farm near Crawfordsville, Georgia. Sickly all his life, Stephens never weighed more than 100 pounds, but he served for 16 years as a US senator from Georgia. In 1858, Stephens retired from politics, but he was unanimously chosen to be vice president of the Confederacy in 1861. *Harper's Weekly* described his voice as "shrill and unpleasant," but called his speeches "eloquent and practical." In 1882, Stephens was elected governor of Georgia.

On April 14, 1865, actor John Wilkes Booth, 26, assassinated President Lincoln at Ford's Theatre in Washington, DC. Six days later, the US War Department used this photograph on a Wanted poster, offering a $50,000 reward for Booth and $25,000 each for his conspirators, John H. Surratt Jr. and David C. "Davey" Herold. Surratt's mother, Mary Surratt, was hanged on July 7, 1865, as their conspirator, along with Herold and two others.

West Point graduate and veteran Plains Indian fighter James Ewell Brown "Jeb" Stuart was one of the most famous Confederate cavalrymen. Stuart helped capture abolitionist John Brown at Harper's Ferry, Virginia, but then resigned his US Army commission to become colonel of the 1st Virginia Cavalry. Promoted to brigadier general, Stuart commanded Gen. Robert E. Lee's cavalry. In 1864, Stuart was mortally wounded at Yellow Tavern near Richmond, Virginia.

Thomas Jonathon Jackson, a West Point graduate, commanded Virginia Military Academy cadets guarding abolitionist John Brown at his execution in 1859. In 1861, during the First Battle of Bull Run, or First Manassas, in Manassas Junction, Virginia, Confederate brigadier general Jackson was dubbed "Stonewall." Fellow brigadier general Barnard E. Bee exclaimed, "Look, there stands Jackson like a stone wall." Unfortunately, Jackson died from three shots of friendly fire from the 18th North Carolina Infantry.

STONEWALL JACKSON.

Without formal military training, Nathan Bedford Forrest became a leading Confederate cavalry leader and tactician. In 1861, Bedford enlisted as a private and rose to general, commanding Forrest's 3rd Tennessee Cavalry. After the war, Forrest became president of the Selma, Marion & Memphis Railroad. In 1869, General Forrest joined a Confederate veterans' secret society, the Ku Klux Klan, and became grand wizard. Later, Forrest renounced his participation.

State and national politician James Fleming Fagan was stepson of the Arkansas state treasurer Samuel Adams, whose image graced the $10 Arkansas treasury notes during the Civil War. In 1861, Fagan raised the 1st Arkansas Infantry, which lost 45 percent of its men during the Battle of Shiloh, Tennessee. The 1st Arkansas Infantry had 33 Southern Cross of Honor recipients, which were the Confederate Medal of Honor. Lacking funds, the Confederacy minted few medals. In 1862, Fagan led his Arkansas Division in the Trans-Mississippi Theatre during Price's Missouri Raid of 1864.

A lawyer prior to the war, John Singleton Mosby fought with the 1st Virginia Cavalry at the First Battle of Bull Run, Virginia, in 1861. In 1862, Mosby scouted for Gen. James Ewell Brown "Jeb" Stuart and Gen. Robert E. Lee. A loyal Democrat, Mosby formed a regiment of ruthless partisan rangers in 1863, but turned Republican after the war and befriended Ulysses S. Grant, who appointed him US consul to Hong Kong, in 1878.

In 1833, Sterling Price married Martha Head on her father's Randolph County, Missouri, farm. They raised seven children, two whom died in infancy, in Chariton County, Missouri. From 1846 to 1848, Price fought in the Mexican War while Martha managed their farm. Price was governor of Missouri from 1853 to 1857, and major general of the Missouri State Guard from 1861 to 1862, before serving in the Confederate State Army from 1862 to 1865.

During the war, Martha Head Price resided in Texas, while Gen. Sterling Price fought with their sons, Gen. Edwin Waller Price and Col. Celsus Price. Compassionate toward wounded soldiers on either side, Sterling Price was affectionately known as "Old Pap." He died in 1867, after returning from self-imposed exile in Mexico. Martha died of pneumonia at her son Edwin's Dalton, Missouri, home in 1870. In 1915, Keytesville, Missouri, unveiled the Gen. Sterling Price Monument in Price Memorial Park, built with $5,000 worth of Senate appropriations and private donations.

In 1858, Joseph Orville "Jo" Shelby married his second cousin, Elizabeth Nancy "Bettie" Shelby, in Waverly, Missouri. In 2011, their wedding was re-enacted during Waverly's Civil War Heritage Festival. Shelby, a wealthy slaveholder, business owner, and inventor, became a Confederate brigadier general during the war. Refusing to surrender, Shelby and about 600 men relocated to Mexico after the war. In 1969, *The Undefeated*, starring John Wayne, was loosely based on their actions.

In 1862, Brig. Gen. Simon Bolivar Buckner Sr. became the first Confederate general to surrender an army when he accepted this demand from Brig. Gen. Ulysses S. Grant: "No terms except unconditional and immediate surrender can be accepted." Grant was nicknamed "Unconditionally Surrender" Grant, playing off his initials, U.S. Grant, and Buckner was dubbed "Simon the Poet" for his fondness for writing poetry. Later, Buckner served as 30th Kentucky governor from 1887 to 1891, and then ran for the vice president on the ticket of former Union general John M. Palmer in 1896. Lieutenant General Buckner died in 1914, as the last Confederate officer ranked higher than a brigadier general.

GEN. BUCKNER.

Imprisoned for shooting a man during a duel, William Lowndes Yancey was a slave owner and a state and national politician in Alabama before joining the Confederacy. In the 1850s, Yancey was dubbed the "Orator of Secession." During the Civil War, Jefferson Davis, as president of the Confederacy, sent Yancey to Europe to gain acknowledgment of the Southern states' right to independence. In 1862–1863, Yancey frequently criticized the Davis administration in the Confederate States Senate.

Kentucky manufacturer John Hunt Morgan led the 2nd Kentucky Cavalry on daring operations against railroads and supply trains. In July 1863, General Morgan and his "Rough Riders" fought at Corydon, the only battle in Indiana, before raiding Ohio, where Morgan and 28 of his command were captured and imprisoned in Ohio Penitentiary. After escaping through a tunnel, General Morgan raided through Kentucky, but was killed in September 1864, after refusing to surrender near Greenville, Tennessee.

In 1821, Patience Monroe Bishop married fellow Virginian Gustavus Adolphus Parsons. Moving to Missouri in 1835, they raised nine children in Jefferson City. Their 16-year-old son, Lt. Gustavus Adolphus Parsons Jr., joined Pindall's 9th Missouri Battalion of Sharp Shooters and died of disease in Van Buren, Arkansas, in December 1862. In 1865, another son, Gen. Mosby Monroe Parsons, and their son-in-law, Col. Austin M. Standish, were killed in Mexico after the Confederacy had surrendered.

Confederate general Mosby Monroe Parsons was a Missouri politician, a Mexican War veteran, and the Civil War commander of the 6th Division, Missouri State Guard. In 1853, Parsons' wife, Mary Wells Parsons died following the birth of their only daughter, Josephine, who passed away one month later. Stephen Kearney Parsons (right), who was only two years old when his mother died, was named after Mexican War general Stephen Watts Kearney. In 1873, Kearney Parsons became sheriff of Jefferson City.

On October 21, 1861, forty-nine original Missouri government members met in the Masonic Hall in Neosho, Missouri to hear Sen. M.C. Goodlett introduce his bill, "An act to dissolve the political connection between the State of Missouri with [*sic*] the United States of America." Thomas H. Murray (right), Clerk of the House, announced the bill's passing. Lieutenant Colonel Murray fought with the 4th Missouri State Guard Volunteer Infantry and the 11th Missouri Infantry.

In 1861, Jeremiah Vardeman Cockrell joined the Missouri State Guard and fought at Carthage, Wilson's Creek, and Lexington, Missouri. In August 1862, Cockrell procured additional Confederate recruits during the Battle of Lone Jack, Missouri. During Gen. Sterling Price's Missouri Raid of 1864, Cockrell was shot by a minié ball, which he kept in a snuffbox until his death in 1915, in Texas, where he had been a lawyer and politician.

In January 1861, Col. John Q. Burbridge organized the 1st Missouri Infantry. In June 1861, Maj. Gen. John Stevens Bowen (shown here) formed the 1st Missouri Infantry in Memphis from the 2nd St. Louis Missouri Volunteer Militia, which had been captured the month before at Camp Jackson by Gen. Nathaniel Lyon. Burbridge's infantry was renamed the 2nd Missouri when it was discovered that Bowen, who outranked Burbridge, had formed his regiment.

In 1825, 19-year-old Mathew Fontaine Maury joined the US Navy. Maury, called the "Pathfinder of the Sea," plotted oceans and recorded navigation methods using currents, winds, and meteorology. A native-Virginian, Maury joined the Confederacy and established the naval Submarine Battery Service in Richmond, which developed underwater explosives. Maury spent most of the war in England and acquired ships and supplies, earning a $3,000 price on his head. After returning from exile in Mexico, Maury became a professor of meteorology at the Virginia Military Institute.

Lewis Hancock Kennerly, 29, and his brothers, Samuel Augustin Kennerly, 21, and James Amadee Kennerly, 18, joined the 1st Missouri Infantry, commanded by their brother-in-law, Gen. John S. Bowen. During the Battle of Baker's Creek, Mississippi, in 1863, Samuel was severely wounded and left on the field for dead, but he survived, only to die a year later at Lovejoy's Station, Georgia. Gen. Francis M. Cockrell said of him, "Kennerly was a most fearless, cheerful, and determined officer."

In 1861, James Madison McCown killed Unionist Marshall "Marsh" Foster during a political meeting in Warrensburg, Missouri. McCown quickly enlisted with his sons, William Henry "Billy" McCown and James Sanford "Samp" McCown, while 13-year-old Charles Calhoun McCown followed along. By 1862, James McCown (left) commanded the 5th Missouri Infantry. Meanwhile, Marsh Foster's brother, Emory S. Foster, burned the McCown house with the help of the 7th Missouri Cavalry. More than 20 years later, Billy McCown was murdered in yet another retaliation for Foster's death.

In 1861, Dr. Andrew C. Atkeson, 52, along with his sons, Alonzo Atkeson, 23, and William Hamilton Atkeson, 16, and his nephew, Barnett James Atkeson, 22, joined the 5th Missouri Infantry. Alonzo died at Baker's Creek (Champion Hill), Mississippi, in 1863, and Barnett (pictured here) died during the Battle of Franklin, Tennessee, in 1864. Andrew's brother, Lewis A. Atkinson, a Union chaplain with the 91st Ohio Infantry, was wounded during the Battle of Opequon, or Third Winchester, Virginia, in 1864.

Francis Marion Cockrell was a Warrensburg, Missouri, attorney, Confederate State Guard Militia leader, and colonel of the 2nd Missouri Infantry, which formed in Springfield in 1862. Marching his troops into battle to the beat of "Dixie," Cockrell became brigadier general and later served 30 years in the US Senate. On Cockrell's 70th birthday, on October 1, 1904, he gave the address during the unveiling of the Confederate Soldier's Monument in Liberty, Missouri.

In 1861, Benjamin G. Dysart became surgeon under Col. James McCown of the 5th Missouri Infantry. The infantry suffered high losses during most engagements, including the Battle of Corinth, in 1862, where 44 percent of the men were lost. Many stories are told of Dysart's personal bravery as surgeon to Gen. Francis M. Cockrell's brigade. After the war, Dr. Dysart had an extensive medical practice in Paris, Missouri. Dysart became vice president of the Missouri State Board of Health in 1901, and he died three years later.

Born in Franklin County, Tennessee, in 1843, Ellen Lipscomb was the daughter of abolitionist Granville Lipscomb and his third wife, Jane Breeden, of Virginia. Ellen Lipscomb's nine-year marriage to Confederate major James Isom Gardner left her a widowed mother of four children when he died in 1880. In 1891, Ellen's older brother, David Lipscomb, co-founded Nashville Bible School, which became David Lipscomb University following his death in 1918 and then became Lipscomb University in 1994.

West Point graduate Leonidas Polk founded the University of the South in Sewanee, Tennessee. He was also the Episcopal Diocese of Louisiana's first bishop and an Episcopal missionary bishop to the Republic of Texas. He was the uncle of Confederate brigadier general Lucius Polk, of the 15th Arkansas Regiment, and the second cousin of Pres. James K. Polk. Gen. Leonidas Polk, called "the Fighting Bishop," was killed during the Atlanta Campaign in 1864.

Jubal Anderson Early was a West Point graduate, Virginia attorney, and veteran of the Seminole, Mexican, and Civil Wars. Although Early strongly opposed secession, "Old Jube" joined the Confederacy as a colonel of the 24th Virginia Infantry. After the war, Early became involved in the Louisiana State Lottery Company, dubbed "The Serpent", a legal gambling operation meant to spur the Southern economy. He was also president of the Southern Historical Association, which promoted the military reputations of former Confederate generals.

Joseph Wheeler was a West Point graduate and an Alabama lawyer and Congressman. Wheeler was assigned to the Regiment of Mounted Rifles in the New Mexico Territory in 1860. While escorting a wagon train from Hannibal, Missouri, to Fort Craig, an ambulance carrying a mother and new baby was attacked by Indians. Wheeler charged them, guns blazing, earning the nickname "Fightin' Joe." The next year, he joined the Confederacy. During the Spanish-American War in 1898, Maj. Gen. Wheeler commanded the Cavalry Division of the Cuban Expeditionary Force, which included future 26th president Theodore "Teddy" Roosevelt and his Rough Riders.

On March 4, 1861, the day of President Lincoln's first inauguration, pro-Southern "Minute Man" James M. "Jim" Quinlan replaced the US flag on the federal courthouse in St. Louis with a specially designed secessionist flag. In June, Quinlan, 28, enlisted in the 1st Missouri Infantry in Memphis and was appointed commissary sergeant. He was wounded during the battles of Shiloh and Vicksburg.

Tennessean Benjamin E. McCulloch was born in 1811, one of 12 children. Following David "Davy" Crocket to Texas in 1835, McCulloch fought in the Battle of San Jacinto with Sam Houston. McCulloch was a Texas Ranger and a politician who became a "49er" during the California Gold Rush in 1849. On March 7, 1862, Brigadier General McCulloch was killed leading a division in Arkansas during the Battle of Elkhorn Tavern, which was known as the Battle of Pea Ridge to the Yankees. McCulloch County, Texas, is named for him.

In 1861, Confederate first lieutenant John E. Josey joined the 1st Infantry Regiment State Troops (Arkansas), which became the 15th Arkansas Infantry (Cleburne's-Polk's-Josey's) with Josey as colonel. This regiment fought from the battles of Shiloh and Chickamauga to Richmond, Kentucky, and Atlanta. Josey was captured in 1864, on the St. Francis River in Arkansas, and imprisoned at Camp Chase in Columbus, Ohio. Josey was exchanged in February 1865, and died the next year of yellow fever in Osceola, Florida.

Nine

The "Brown Water" Navy

Within two weeks of Lincoln's assassination on April 14, 1865, the SS *Sultana* exploded on the Mississippi River, but the tragedy of the wooden paddle wheeler received little lasting attention in the wake of Gen. Robert E. Lee's surrender at Appomattox Courthouse on April 9. The US government offered *Sultana* captain James Cass Mason $5 per enlisted man and $10 per officer for transporting them home. On April 21, the two-year-old *Sultana* left New Orleans, en route to St. Louis, with 85 crew members and 95 passengers. In Vicksburg, about 2,400 desperate Federal soldiers swarmed her decks. Recently released from Confederate prisons such as Cahawba, in Alabama, and Andersonville, in Georgia, the soldiers were weak, malnourished, ill, and desperate for home. On April 26, at Helena, Arkansas, the *Sultana*'s last photograph shows her overcrowded decks. That night, at 2:00 a.m., near the Hen and Chicken Islands north of Memphis, the boilers exploded. Almost 1,700 drowned, burned to death, or died from their injuries. A few survivors formed the Sultana Survivors Society, holding annual meetings for years.

David Dixon Porter, who began his naval career at 16, served in the Mexican and Civil Wars. Admiral Porter's fleet contained several ironclads, including USS *Lafayette*, USS *Benton*, and USS *Pittsburgh*, and timber-clad boats like USS *General Price*. Porter commanded the North Atlantic Blockading Squadron during the last months of the war. Five naval ships were named in honor of Admiral Porter and his father, Commodore David Porter.

USS *Lafayette* was built in 1848 as a side-wheel merchant steamer. Beginning in 1861, the Army utilized *Lafayette* as a quartermaster ship until her conversion to an ironclad gunboat and ram in September 1862. Adm. David D. Porter used the *Lafayette* against the Confederates at Vicksburg and during the Red River Expedition in Louisiana. She is shown here between 1863 and 1865, decorated with flags on the Mississippi River.

In 1861, James Buchanan Eads converted a catamaran snagboat into USS *Benton*. This unidentified sailor was one of her 176 crewmen. *Benton,* the largest Union ironclad, participated in most Federal operations on the Mississippi River and its tributaries. In 1862, Capt. William Gwin and nine *Benton* crewmen died securing a Yazoo River, Mississippi, landing location for Gen. William T. Sherman. Later, five *Benton* crew members received Medals of Honor.

Robert Benecke joined the 18th Missouri Infantry in 1861, but after a medical discharge, he began a photography business with Hermann E. Hoelke in St. Louis. Together, Benecke and Hoelke took first prize for stereographs and photographic views at the St. Louis Fair in 1867 and 1868. Benecke created this stereograph of the Eagle Packet Company and steamboats in the late 1860s. The Eagle Packet Company ran from St. Louis to Alton and Grafton, Illinois.

The *New Era* ferry was built in 1856 and was turned into the timber-clad gunboat USS *Saint Mary* in 1861. Renamed USS *Essex,* she was damaged during the capture of Fort Henry, Tennessee, in 1862. This photograph was taken while the *Essex* was coaling in Baton Rouge in July 1862. Commodore William D. Porter upgraded *Essex* into one of the most powerful ironclads afloat. In April 1865, *Essex* rescued 60 people after the SS *Sultana* explosion.

Joining the US Navy in 1823, 15-year-old William D. Porter followed in the footsteps of his father, Commodore David Porter, and his younger brother, Adm. David Dixon Porter. After Commodore William Porter destroyed the ironclad CSS *Arkansas* with USS *Saint Mary* in 1862, he renamed the *Saint Mary* the *Essex* after his father's War of 1812 ship. Scottish-born 19th-century American engraver and portrait painter Alexander Hay Ritchie produced this engraving of William D. Porter.

USS *Pittsburg* was one of seven "city" or Cairo-class ironclad gunboats built by James B. Eads in Carondelet, Missouri, in 1861. They were also called "Pook's Turtles," after their designer, Samuel M. Pook, and for their low, wide waterline profile. All the city-class ironclads began as steamboat paddle wheelers, with the exception of USS *Mound City*, which had a screw propeller.

Engineer James B. Eads supervised the construction of USS *Mound City*, USS *Cincinnati*, and USS *Cairo* by the Hambleton & Collier Company in Mound City, Illinois. In December 1862, *Cairo*, commanded by Thomas O. Selfridge Jr., struck two torpedoes (now known as mines) and sank. For 102 years, she sat on the bottom of the Yazoo River before being raised in 1964, restored, and displayed at the Vicksburg National Military Park.

"City" class ironclad gunboat USS *Carondelet* is shown here, tarped while moored to the bank. In 1865, *Carondelet* was decommissioned and her hull became a wharf boat in Gallipolis, Ohio. In 1873, a flood pulled her 130 miles downstream, and she sank at Manchester Island, Ohio. In 1982, author Clive Cussler and his National Underwater and Marine Agency (NUMA) located the 109-year-old shipwreck, but a dredge boat destroyed it two days before Cussler arrived.

These USS *St. Louis* sailors wear the typical black silk neckerchiefs. Black sweat rags were used because they showed less dirt. Seamen began wearing flat hats in 1852 but discontinued the use on April 1, 1963, because the cost and availability of materials became prohibitive. Originally, the hatband, or "talley," displayed the sailor's unit or ship name, but it was replaced in 1941 with "US Navy" for security reasons.

By the middle of 1862, the Union Army and Union Navy realized the need for co-operations to control the western rivers. Brig. Gen. Alfred Washington Ellet organized a new unit called the Mississippi Marine Brigade, which contained six infantry companies, four cavalry companies, and one artillery company. Ellet traveled aboard the flagship *Autocrat*. The men were permanently stationed aboard the unarmed steamboats *Baltic*, *John Raine*, *B.J. Adams*, *Diana*, and *Fairchild*, which were attached to Ellet's Ram Fleet.

Mary Jane Davis Whitehead was the wife of Onesimus Weldon Whitehead, who joined the 35th Illinois Infantry at Dry Point, Illinois, in March 1861. In July, First Sergeant Whitehead transferred to the Mississippi Marine Brigade and relocated to St. Louis. After the war, Onesimus and Mary moved to Michigan, where they applied for a Veteran's pension when Onesimus became disabled in 1875. Mary applied for a widow's pension in 1884.

Swedish immigrant John Ericsson, shown here in 1862, was one of the most creative engineers and inventors of the 19th century. The US Navy recognized his talents and lured him to America in the 1840s. Ericsson designed and produced the ironclad USS *Monitor* with a rotating turret. Completed in 101 days, *Monitor* had over 40 mechanisms aboard with original patents. Three Navy ships are named in Ericsson's honor.

Livestock and fowl were brought aboard for meals while at war, but they were not the only animals at sea. During the Civil War, sailors often acquired pets and took them on their ship. Dogs, often puppies, were the most frequent pets. Some dogs served a practical purpose, such as hunting when the sailors went ashore. These "mascots" provided companionship and entertainment for the entire crew.

Ten

150th Battle of Wilson's Creek Anniversary Commemoration

Re-enactors chat near the tents of the 25 sutlers who came to sell their wares at the 150th Battle of Wilson's Creek Anniversary Re-enactment. Sutlers came from 13 states: Alabama, Arkansas, Florida, Georgia, Illinois, Indiana, Iowa, Kansas, Kentucky, Ohio, Missouri, Tennessee, and Wisconsin. The sutlers included 96 Storehouse, with period fabric, Adler's Drygoods, Allen's Laurel Hill Sutlery, Barrancas Mercantile, Border States Leather, Carrico's Leather, Civil War Lady, Cool Creek Forge, Coon River Mercantile, Dixie Gun Works, Fall Creek Sutlery, Hansen's Mercantile, Kentwood Sutlery, Ladies and Gentlemen's Emporium, Ladies Parlor, Lady in Black, Ortega Traders, P. Palmer Dry Goods, Rum Creek Sutler, Snow Creek Boots, Southern Family Impressions, The Sutler of Fort Scott, The Lantern Man, The Paper Lady, and Village Tinsmithing Works. James Country Mercantile also repaired weapons. Jack's Powder Keg ammunition company from Kisatchie, Louisiana, supplied the powder for the battle re-enactments, and the Wilson's Creek National Battlefield Foundation covered the cost. (Courtesy of Steve Ross.)

In 1854, Diersberg began as a general store, selling baking products, fabric, clothing, hardware, and other staples in Creve Coeur, Missouri. Now, fourth-generation owner Robert Diersberg manages 25 stores. His brother, James, restored Hermann Farm, a 19th-century farm in Hermann, Missouri, where a skirmish took place in 1864. Hermann Farm opened in September 2011, as a living history museum complete with old-time farm chores (Courtesy of Steven Titus.)

Sandi Swift (left), of Osage, Iowa, and Joy Melcher, of St. Charles, Missouri, believe that dressing patriotically is a wonderful way to commemorate the 150th Civil War anniversary events. Joy and Sandi have been re-enacting for over 20 years and even raised their children as re-enactors. Joy designs period clothing, which she sells at www.CivilWarLady.com and at history shows and re-enactments, where she takes 200–300 ready-made gowns for sale. (Courtesy of the author.)

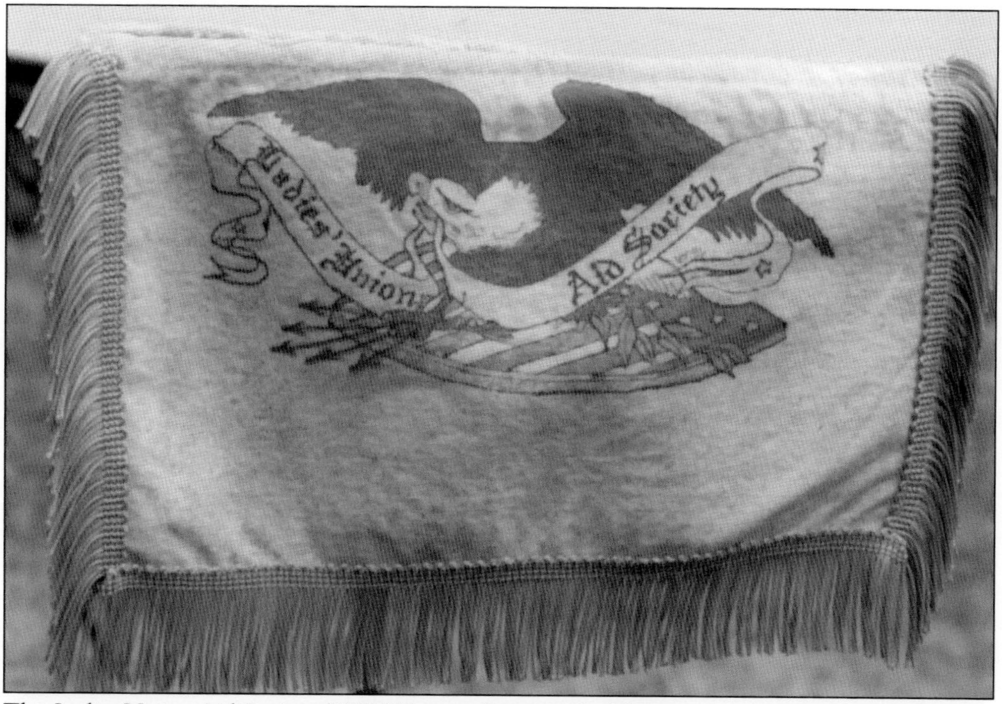

This Ladies Union Aid Society (LUAS) banner hung in the Union camp during the re-enactment. The LUAS began in St. Louis in 1861, with members in other Northern towns as well. The members rolled bandages and collected donation boxes and financial gifts while visiting the wounded in hospitals and on battlefields. Adeline Couzins, wounded at Vicksburg, was one of the few LUAS pension recipients. (Courtesy of Steven Titus.)

This beautiful flag represents the battalion flag from the 1st US Infantry. On August 10, 1861, Brig. Gen. Joseph Plummer's battalion of the 1st US Infantry Regiment fought in the cornfield at the John Ray house during the Battle of Wilson's Creek. Brigadier General Plummer was wounded at Wilson's Creek, but lived another year, until he was killed on August 9, 1862, during the Battle of Corinth, Mississippi. (Courtesy of Steven Titus.)

The banjo and fiddle were the most popular instruments during the war. In the evening—pressures of war permitting—men crowded near the campfire while the regiment musicians played the accordion, banjo, guitar, or harmonica. Confederate general James E.B. "Jeb" Stuart was so fond of banjo music that he kept his own regimental banjo player, an orderly named Sam Sweeney, who was the younger brother of the "inventor" of the five-string banjo, Joel Sweeney. (Courtesy of Steven Titus.)

These re-enactors portray a drummer and other members of a Confederate Artillery Battery. At the beginning of the war, Confederate musicians, farriers, and blacksmiths were paid $13 a month, just $2 more than a private, but $182 less than a colonel. Musicians were often detached from their regiments and assigned to medical units as nurses, where they were required to attend to the wounded on the field. The Union Army had an estimated 40,000 musicians. (Courtesy of Steven Titus.)

Re-enactors fire off a reproduction cannon during one of the Battle of Wilson's Creek 150th Anniversary's five re-enactments. The spectators were awed by explosions, smoke, and flames from the artillery blast. The smell of black powder and the smoke rings drifting across the field added to the authenticity of the event, as did the frantically shouted orders and thundering hooves of horses. In the evenings, night firing demonstrations were performed. The re-enactments were the highlight of the three-day event, which will be remembered for years to come. (Both, courtesy of Steve Ross.)

INDEX